Essays on History and Literature

Edited by <u>Robert H. Bremner</u>

Essays on History
and Literature

Daniel Aaron

Edward Lurie

Stow Persons

Russel B. Nye

OHIO STATE UNIVERSITY PRESS

For Rhea and Marion Dulles

INTRODUCTION

This volume, like the conference at which the essays were originally presented, is intended to honor Foster Rhea Dulles on his advancement from professor to professor emeritus at the Ohio State University. Perhaps only academicians would deem subjecting a friend to a series of scholarly lectures a suitable way of observing such an occasion. Professor Dulles' colleagues, although aware of the irony, chose that method of paying tribute to his services to the University and to the historical profession. Remembering Professor Dulles' concern with history as a literary art, the Graduate School and the Department of History invited four literary and intellectual historians to the Ohio State University campus to discuss topics bearing on the relationship of literature to history. One of the speakers, Daniel Aaron, had been a colleague of Professor Dulles at the start of the latter's academic career. Aside from noting this fortunate circumstance, sponsors and speakers refrained from memorializing the guest of honor. His contributions to American social history and the history of American foreign policy seemed too abundant and well known to require celebration. Professor Dulles retired from teaching in the midst, rather than at the close, of his activity as a student and author. The essays here assembled are addressed, therefore, not only to him but to all who share his interest in the writing of history.

All of the essays deal with the analysis, evaluation, organization, and presentation of historical evidence. They do not treat the newest problems of historiography—computer-assisted research and data-processing techniques—but the omission of these problems does not signify indifference to contemporary trends of historical scholarship. Literature remains a source and resource of history whether the writer's approach is quantitative or impressionistic. Historians cannot ignore the poetry, fiction, and drama of a period any more than they can pass over the state papers, diaries, letters, newspaper editorials, pamphlets, annual reports, and other documents of the time. Nearly every historian uses literary allusions to enliven and adorn his pages. Lines of verse, fictional characters, themes of novels and plays, like the styles and subjects of pictures, statues, and monuments, all influence the writer's conception of an age.

Regardless of the use or misuse historians make of literary evidence, imaginative literature is a personal statement of values. It seldom purports to be an accurate chronicle of events, and the judgment it passes on the motives and consequences of human conduct represents, not a consensus, but the author's individual conviction. The literature of a given period is part of the contemporary testimony about the problems and meaning of the era. It may prove indispensable, useful, or of only marginal value to historians of the period. The import of the testimony resides in the quality of the witness and the susceptibility or sensitivity of the historian-evaluator. The question is not whether historians ought to consult literary evidence but how they should employ it to discover and illumine the shape of the past.

If the question has a single, definitive answer, the essays in this book do not provide it. Although intended to be instructive, the essays are more cautionary and illustrative than prescriptive. The authors offer advice and guidance; but, instead of laying down rules, they encourage readers to seek their own solutions. Daniel Aaron, drawing on his experience in studying the American literary Left in the 1930's, discusses problems—especially those of motivation— encountered in writing about the recent past while many of the actors are still alive. The situations Professor Aaron considers require attention because, as he reminds us, all history was once contemporary history. Edward Lurie also seeks to break "the web of deception" "contemporaries" spin about their times. He argues that there are other and more informative sources for understanding American intellectual life in the middle and late years of the nineteenth century than *The Education of Henry Adams*. Professor Lurie advances an interpretation of nineteenth-century American cultural history that recognizes the persistent association of intellectuals with men of affairs and draws attention to the "urge to conserve and order cultural activity" common to both groups. Stow Persons treats the American intellectual elite of the nineteenth century as members of a distinct social class, the gentry, whose habits, functions, and commitments set it apart from both the social-economic elite and the populistic mass. Professor Persons' essay might be entitled "The Social Origins of the Genteel Tradition." He uses conventional sources of intellectual history to clarify social structure and employs the methods of social history to explain "the disciplined and cautious tone of gentry culture." More explicitly than the other contributors, Russel Nye reviews the usefulness of literature to history and explores similarities and differences between the two disciplines. Through the "vital quality of imaginative evocation," Professor Nye concludes, history recreates and literature renews "the universal elements of human experience."

For those who wish to pursue the inquiry beyond the range of this volume, Margaret E. Kahn and George P. Schoyer have compiled a bibliography of books and articles on the use of literature in research in American history. The compilers and the editor trust that the list will prove helpful, and hope that it will often need to be lengthened.

ROBERT H. BREMNER

CONTENTS

DANIEL AARON
*The Treachery of Recollection: The Inner and the
Outer History*   3

EDWARD LURIE
*American Scholarship: A Subjective Interpretation of
Nineteenth-Century Cultural History*   31

STOW PERSONS
The Origins of the Gentry   83

RUSSEL B. NYE
History and Literature: Branches of the Same Tree   123

*A Selected Bibliography on the Use of Literature in
Research in American History, compiled by
Margaret E. Kahn and George P. Schoyer*   163

Notes on the Contributors   181

Index   185

DANIEL AARON

The Treachery of Recollection:
The Inner and the Outer History

DANIEL AARON

The Treachery of Recollection:
The Inner and the Outer History

> *The situation of our time*
> *Surrounds us like a baffling crime.*
>
> —*W. H. Auden, The Double Man*

What I propose to do in this paper is to raise certain
problems and to ask certain questions about the
writing of contemporary history. More particularly,
I shall refer to events that have taken place during
my own lifetime and that have involved a number of
people who are still alive. These men and women (to
narrow the scope of my discourse even further) were
or are writers and intellectuals, and the events I shall
mention belong to the history of literary radicalism
during the 1920's and 30's. Since these remarks
might be subtitled "Some Belated Conclusions about
Writers and Political Movements," and since they
also might be considered a personal documentation of
T. S. Eliot's unconsoling reflections on history, my
approach to the subject will be necessarily autobiographical.

I

As interest keeps mounting in the thirties, a number of special studies are appearing on the politics

and culture of this period—the first trickles of an impending flood. Already some of the writers and intellectuals who came of age between two world wars have written their memoirs in whole or in part, and the recollections of other hitherto reticent men and women will doubtless follow.*

This sudden burst of reminiscence comes a little tardily. Until a short time ago, scholars and writers rather studiedly avoided the thirties; the depression decade, in contrast to the supposedly apolitical twenties, became one to forget or to denigrate. Veterans of those embattled years had retired to lick their wounds or to brood over their disenchantment, publicly or privately; and writers who had once thrilled to dubious Soviet statistics or had mourned the defeats of the Spanish Republicans now dropped old political loyalties with huge relief, happy to be restored once again to the stupid but unwittingly prophetic community. Some flagellated themselves in print; some trivialized their adventures in nonconformity, dismissing their radical enthusiasms as youthful aberrations or follies and joking about episodes that once had kindled a passionate concern.

* Floyd Dell, Max Eastman, Joseph Freeman, Edmund Wilson, Dwight MacDonald, to name only a few, have personalized this period. Recently published or soon to appear are the autobiographical accounts of Granville Hicks, Malcolm Cowley, Matthew Josephson, and Alfred Kazin—and this is only the beginning.

4

All in all, the forties and fifties saw a good deal of soul-searching, breast-beating, and mutual recrimination.

This wholesale rejection of old convictions need not have been carried on so masochistically; but candid retrospection was discouraged after the war by a political and cultural assault on what came to be stigmatized as the liberal fallacies of the thirties. Not only Marxism was attacked. All the liberal clichés fell under the postwar ban, with former leftists presiding over the autopsy of the radical-liberal corpse. These same people and their disciples took pains to announce in literary quarterlies, in classrooms, in summer conferences for young writers, that the old formulas were hopelessly inadequate. Few had a good word to say for the popular left-wing writers of the thirties or the literary forms and styles these writers had used to convey their angry or hopeful messages. The new line was to dismiss them as primitives, clumsy practitioners who simplified art, advocated naïve social cures, and sentimentalized corrupt human nature.

The new literary stance was conservative, formal, and noncommittal. Writers and intellectuals too young to have remembered either the exhilaration or anguish of the thirties accepted the afterthoughts and reconsiderations of their elders, both in politics and in art. At least it seemed so to many critics in the 1950's who found the new writing disciplined and restrained and a little flat. They dubbed the postwar generation, perhaps unfairly, the "conservative," the "timid," the "anxious" generation—a far cry from the writers and intellectuals who once held powerful convictions and acted upon them.

With the deflation of McCarthyism, curiosity (especially in academic circles) about the former radicals whose names had appeared in the reports of Congressional investigating committees began to manifest itself. An ostensibly apolitical "beat" generation discovered some of its ancestors in the "Bottom Dog" writers of the depression, and college students, perhaps surfeited with bitter-sweet chronicles of the "Lost Generation" era, started to ask questions about literary life during the Roosevelt years. Why did this particular writer become involved with the left movement? And why did he or she break away? Were many writers involved? How important was the influence of communism on writers? How many were bona fide revolutionaries and how many merely rebels, indignant about all injustices?

These were some of the questions I asked myself in the mid-fifties when I began to study the American literary left movement and to investigate the political activities and beliefs of writers who played a part in it. What follows will be reconsiderations of the problems and difficulties anyone faces who seeks to set down the internal as well as external history of the recent past and who wants to tell the story while many of the actors are still alive.

II

Aldous Huxley once said that only the dead are consistent. The historian of the past confines his attentions to the "consistent" dead who are safely under the ground and therefore is spared certain embarassments that he may not appreciate until he turns his attention to the inconsistent living. His dead subjects belong to the public domain. He can write about them with impunity, unless, of course, the manuscripts and letters are guarded by solicitous heirs or supervised by property-conscious executors who place stipulations upon their use.

Yet even with these obstacles, the historian of the past is free to probe into the lives of the departed with the comfortable feeling that they are not likely to talk back or sue him for libel. He can judge them, speculate about their motives, deal with the most intimate and delicate moments of their careers; and he can do this in the knowledge that they are beyond pain. In other words, writing about a man who *was*

7

rather than about a man who *is* encourages candor. The historian or biographer is able to arrange his subject in a variety of poses, treat him clinically or irreverently, psychoanalyze him, or make him a text for a sermon.

This latitude is denied to historians who write about their living contemporaries, but in compensation they enjoy obvious advantages that historians of the past are necessarily deprived of—most notably, the chance to see and to talk with many of the principal actors. The adage "Dead men tell no tales," is as relevant for historians, literary or otherwise, as it is for pirates; and in my own case, the prospect of talking with live authors (who have many tales to tell if they can be induced to talk) was an alluring one. All of us at one time or another have daydreamed about reversing the Time Machine: of waking up, for example, in the eighteenth century, like the hero of Henry James's unfinished novel, *The Sense of the Past;* of eavesdropping on the unreported conversations between Melville and Hawthorne as they strolled in the Berkshires, or discussing "Song of Myself" with Walt Whitman while riding on a Broadway omnibus.

Now it would seem that the historian of the present has less need to resort to such fancies. He can write letters to the people he is connected with. He can visit them, record their statements, extract information from their friends and enemies. Their books and articles are efficiently catalogued, and libraries purchase their papers well before the writers themselves have cashed their last checks. With this plethora of palpable evidence, secrets and mysteries would seem to disappear.

I say would *seem* to, and yet I suspect that anyone who has written about his contemporaries would disagree. He might not say that it is much harder to write about the living than the dead, but he might well assert that it is a different and trickier undertaking and one replete with inhibiting traps and pitfalls. The historian who writes of the past might be likened to a naturalist as he observes and analyzes specimens in a museum or perhaps animals caged in a zoo. The historian of the present resembles rather a hunter stalking his unpredictable quarry in a jungle. And to push the analogy further, in this hunting game, the quarry keeps changing shape. What starts out looking like a rabbit may turn into a porcupine; an elephant is transmogrified into a mouse. To put it still another way: When the investigator tracks down his man (or his woman) some twenty-five to forty-five years after a particular episode, he is not seeing and talking to the same man who wrote the manifesto or who paraded in the picket line or sent a congratulatory

message to the *New Masses* on its anniversary or who
bit another celebrity in the leg during a drunken
party. Or would it be more accurate to say that he
is confronting a different man in the same body, a
man not necessarily the most reliable authority on
his previous self?

Granted that we err in chopping Time arbitrarily
into past, present, and future, that Time flows in
both directions and that there can be no Now uncon-
nected with what was or will be. Nevertheless, what
a person was or did or thought thirty years ago is
past and dead, even if that person is technically
alive. The living relic is his own ancestor; and feeling
a deep familial piety for his defunct historical self,
he indulges in ancestor worship, tidies up embarass-
ing disorders of his dead past, reverently conceals his
own skeleton in a hidden closet. The astute interro-
gator may hear the reverberations of the telltale
heart, but he is also susceptible to misdirection and
perhaps deserves less trust, finally, than the unborn
scholarly detective who will disinter the "truth" long
after the objects of his researches have become
authentic corpses.

In the meantime, the living historian who writes
about his contemporaries may wonder from time to
time whether he has any business raking up the pasts
of people who are still alive. In this age of public

relations, covert investigations, and wholesale viola-
tions of privacy, should the scholar join the pack?
I raise this question, because I was not only concerned with the former opinions and actions of writers
still very much alive, but I was also particularly
interested to learn about their involvement in a political movement retroactively condemned as subver-
sive. What is more, I was approaching them at the
close of the McCarthy period.

Some of the people I hoped to interview were still
in the "Movement," that vague and elastic euphe-
mism for the left; some were politically homeless;
and a few had moved over to the right of Barry
Goldwater. The majority were liberals who had
broken with the "Movement" at various moments during the turbulent thirties. But you will recall that in
Senator McCarthy's heyday, fifteen or more years of
an apolitical existence cut no ice with Congressional
headhunters. We are still uncomfortably close to the
days when writers were "invited" to testify about
their former political affiliations, when prominent
and forgotten people denounced old associates, and
skittish employers dared not hire (or fired) the
blacklisted. Quite obviously in 1956, my own project
—no matter how detached and scholarly and scrupu-
lous my intentions—might ultimately hurt someone.
Why should these writers pour out their hearts to an

outsider engaged in excavating a past they had either forgotten or had no desire to recall?

One of them, whose faith in communism remained strong after half a century, wrote to me in reply to my request for an interview:

I am suspicious of young scholars who set out to make a career out of cannibalizing the history of Communism and Socialism and all social thought in this country, not engaged themselves, observers and critics only, as though they were spies or something. I mean, "who walks without sympathy and passion is walking to his own funeral in a shroud." Something like this was said by Walt Whitman.

His letter, which must have expressed the feelings of a good many other veterans of "the Cause," reminded me of the dialogue between the narrator and the antique owner of the Aspern papers in Henry James's story:

"Do you think it's right to rake up the past?" [she asks].

"I don't feel that I know what you mean by raking it up [he replies]. How can we get at it unless we dig a little? The present has such a rough way of treading it down?"

"Oh I like the past, but I don't like critics," my hostess declared with her hard complacency.

"Neither do I, but I like their discoveries."

"Aren't they mostly lies?"

"The lies are what they sometimes discover," I said, smiling at the quiet impertinence of this. "They often lay bare the truth."

12

"The truth is God's, it isn't man's; we had better leave it alone. Who can judge of it?—who can say?"

Who indeed? The only answer I could offer my correspondent and to others who shared his suspicions was to say that this "cannibalizing" had been going on for some time and that after the mountains of misinformation about the radical movement and the intellectuals, it might be a good thing to get the facts straight, or at least to convey as faithfully as possible what it was like to be alive in those days of political convictions and illusions. This is the job for the historian. If he refuses to deal with his times on the grounds that contemporary history is hardly more than vulgar journalism, then the popularizer and the sensationalist rush in where the historian fears to tread.

For some, my professed concern for "truth" was hardly an inducement to "tell all," especially if this meant dredging up the memory of a youthful gesture or expression of opinion violently at odds with the popular image of the men-now-become-older. One very successful and widely known entrepreneur of letters bluntly refused me permission to quote from some "nonsense" he had written to friends in the early thirties on the grounds that he composed this "bit of childish indignation" when he and his friends "were all off in the head, often because we were starving." Neither he nor his friends were literally starving, of course, but that was his latter-day "vision of the thirties" and his highly improbable explanation for his radical phase.

As it turned out, most of the writers I wanted to see were not so reticent about their left-wing adventures and were prepared to talk with me and to answer questions, if only, perhaps, to dispel legends about themselves and their friends. If they felt any hesitation, it was not so much because of their past or present opinions but simply because the more eminent among them had been pestered by inquirers of all ages and levels. We are living at a time when high-school, college, and graduate students are encouraged to go directly to the source in preparing papers and theses on living men of letters. American writers of any reputation are constantly receiving requests from youthful strangers demanding answers to the most personal questions and even seeking permission to rummage through their private files. It is not hard to understand why these writers, both the remembered and the forgotten, regard students and scholars with mournful misgivings and concoct ingenious schemes to circumvent literary detectives.

For these reasons, and for some yet to be mentioned, writing about one's contemporaries can be as painful as it is challenging. It is bad enough to probe into a person's political or private life like one of Hawthorne's coldhearted Paul Pry's, to enjoy (no matter how deeply repressed) the thrill of digging up the forgotten and the concealed. But the guilty private eye may also be troubled by the very abundance of alleged "facts" that don't reveal as much as they obscure. Are proferred explanations, given in good faith, about why a writer did or did not take a particular stand to be taken at face value? Self-denigration in personal reminiscence is not uncommon, yet few people like to confess low motives for lofty ends; moreover, distance lends enchantment. One learns that squabbles of a generation ago or earlier still divide people no longer politically engaged; that old quarrels still rankle, quarrels seemingly ideological but which may very well have been prompted by professional jealousy, a bad book review, a stolen mistress; and that the autobiographer writing his memoirs in the 1960's may still be settling old scores after an interval of thirty years.

The historian attempting to record a literary war when many of the veterans are still alive exposes himself to the flying pop bottles that threaten any umpire. He pays for his sins of omission, and he may also suffer embarrassment because he knows too much. I have listened to a perfectly rational explanation for an antipathy or a change in heart, knowing

15

all the time that the speaker had withheld or forgotten some crucial fact I had already obtained from another. Because I was steeped in the gossip of the past and familiar with many sides of ancient scandals and debates, I was constantly fearful that I might offend a particular man or woman by telling an unfamiliar version of an episode, or hurt another by inadvertently revealing unwelcome information.

If this solicitude seems unbecoming to the historian, it is the price he pays for the confidence of those he writes about. When he is invited into a man's house, a gesture of qualified acceptance, he subjects himself to subtle pressures. It is not merely the threat of libel suits (a real one in my case) that induces restraint, that tempts him to exclude, to suppress, to be oblique. It is something quite different, something harder to define.

Let us assume that the historian comes to know his subjects after repeated letters and conversations and drinks. They cease to be merely historical figures or ideological abstractions. They become people. And when they talk to him trustfully, when they divulge past indiscretions or drop facts perhaps unimportant in themselves but quite conceivably portentous when added to the questioner's store of information, they take it for granted that the questioner does not intend to crucify them. Having obtained knowledge in such circumstances, the historians may never *intentionally* keep back any relevant fact, but he may find himself writing less sharply, perhaps, than he otherwise would if the writers were merely names or incarnations of literary abstractions.

III

Having reached the stage where the historian has completed his research among the living repositories of the past, what follows? Has he left out some essential piece in the puzzle, neglected an important figure? Has he distorted the picture by blurring contextual relations? Has he relied too much on the testimony of one person, or a single group? These misgivings, which never left me, were intensified after a well-known man of letters wrote to me that although a quotation from one of his letters I had fastened upon might be factually accurate, "It is no more authentic in revealing my position than a single candid camera shot which catches its subject in the midst of a grimace is in revealing his true physiognomy."

Since receiving this comment, I have thought a good deal about his phrase "true physiognomy," and I have wondered whether the portraits of our living

17

or recent contemporaries can ever be more than impressionistic daubs. One would suppose that the historian-painter, with his model seated before him, ought to achieve a recognizable likeness, but the reverse is often true.

Consider the question of factual accuracy. It sometimes turns out that the profusion of historical evidence itself compounds the possibility of error. I have in my possession a long letter from a once popular writer that retells and analyzes certain episodes in his career described in the published memoirs of a former friend. He does not accuse the writer of deliberate falsifying, but he attributes the incorrect allegations and errors of fact in the book to the political point of view of the author at the time he was writing his autobiography. Whether or not my correspondent's strictures are justified, they remind us that no writer enjoys total recall, that every recollection is suspect.

Nor can newspapers always be trusted. In 1935, the *New York Times* reported that the proletarian novelists Jack Conroy and Nelson Algren had driven to Alabama with a committee of writers and had been shot at by some of the local goons. Later, I learned from Conroy that Algren had reneged at the last moment and hadn't gone. This is a trivial example; but if other so-called facts, embalmed in history like flies in amber, are as unreliable, how much more questionable or unascertainable are the conversations and meetings and alcoholic parties recollected in tranquility? How true, really, are the tales from the horse's mouth? Eyewitness accounts of a murder or accident, we are told, often contradict each other. How much more untrustworthy may be the recollections of people who have conscious or unconscious motives for selective remembering or forgetting, who are themselves parties to the events described, whose view of the past is blurred by ignorance, hostility, or sentimentality? And when these murky memories are recorded by imperfect receivers, themselves deaf to finer vibrations, then written history concocted from such sources can become little more than hypotheses about what might have happened.

Would the historian of the present, then, be better advised to skip the interviews, stay aloof from the actors, and write without inhibitions from the published evidence? Might not the story of literary men and radicalism be more profitably and objectively examined twenty-five to fifty years from now, when all the people concerned have vanished, all the autobiographies finished, and all the letters published?

After my long stint of gathering material about living writers—or the recently living—I am left with the uncomfortable feeling that my record of their lives, my explanations for their behavior and motives, are grounded on half-truths and partial evidence. At the same time, I don't think my mistakes or distortions or omissions could have been corrected in every instance by more rigorous methods of research, and I don't think the project was premature.

Every historian must feel occasionally that his results are questionable without entirely discounting them, and the recognition of ambiguities can often be illuminating in itself. I have listed some of the difficulties that beset the historian who seeks to explain his contemporaries. In the remainder of my paper, I should like to show how direct association with the men and women who lived through the twenties and thirties can enlighten as well as perplex him.

IV

A few years ago, Mr. Lewis Mumford observed in a letter to me:

The moving idea during the thirties was not the vision of socialist transformation of our country. What made people join all sorts of movements, from technocracy to communism, from the Douglas plan to socialism, was the desire to repair the broken down machinery of our society and overcome the poverty and misery and fear that visited even the middle classes and the once-affluent professional classes. So badly had the dominant economic and political organiza-

20

tions failed that they were willing to try anything in order
to correct injustices and restore life to our paralyzed economic limbs, as a person stricken with a fatal disease is
willing to try anything, from homeopathy to surgery, provided it promises relief. The spectacle of human suffering
was so widespread and inescapable that only the stupid
or the hard-hearted could accept the existing order as the
last word.

Other contemporaries had stated the same idea more
or less eloquently. But why did particular men and
women join or not join the Communist party? Why
did writers break away from the movement at one
time and not at another? A person's motives may be
as mysterious to himself as to others, but it would
seem on closer inspection that the decision had more
behind it than responsiveness to human suffering.

I should be the last to discount the real despair
of the thirties that fed upon depression conditions or
to play down any more than Mr. Mumford would the
generous indignation excited by poverty and human
callousness. But my interviews and reading lead me
at the same time to a conclusion I cannot document,
but which I nevertheless strongly believe, that some
writers joined or broke from the movement because
of their wives, or for careerist reasons, or because
they read their own inner disturbances into the realities of social dislocation. To put it another way, the
subject matter of politics (left-wing politics in this

case) was often simply the vehicle for nonpolitical emotions and compulsions.

This conviction was reinforced after I had received a letter from Mr. Kenneth Burke, a writer I had read and admired for many years and whom I thought I understood pretty well. I had selected him for special scrutiny, and I had described his response to communism as primarily rational and intellectual rather than religious or emotional. Later, he wrote me that his feelings toward the left movement had not been nearly so detached and whimsical as I had suggested, and he cited one of his poems, published in the *New Masses* (a plea to harness human passions) as an illustration:

Try if you can [he wrote] . . . (so much gets lost between the writing and the written!) imagine it being written, or try to, in an orgy of weeping. For that's exactly how it was written. Analyzing it in later years, I realize that the principle of unification here celebrated was by no means of the political sort that the poem designates on its face. Or, more accurately, the personal, psychological motives that are not there at all, for the reader viewing the poem *ab extra* (as, of course, it should be read, for public aesthetic purposes).

I could cite many other things that I wrote during that period, things involving an order of motives that I know for a fact were implicated, yet do not reveal themselves if read simply on their face.

The points he continued to explicate in this letter

were the profound nonpolitical aspects of his affilia-
tion with the left and the impossibility of solving the
mystery of political commitment. "What is the point
of all this?" his letter concludes.

Simply to state my feeling that, among every man [*sic*]
whose ideas and antics you review, there were many for
whom their political stand was interwoven with many
strands not thus specifically political at all (except in the
sense that one cd. reduce all human relations to politics.)
Yet the merging is so thorough, one would be hard put
whether to say that it is or is not "deeply or religiously
felt." I know it for a fact that the motives involved in my
verses . . . were not reducible to the terms that show on
the face of the poem. In this sense, the politics might be
called a sham. Yet there was no other way to state this
poem, and the political attitude was vitally necessary to
their utterance. In this sense, they might be said to "give
depth" to the political dimension. For some, politics had
very definite sexual tie-ups (normal or perverted); for
others, it meant the alternative to such involvements. For
some it meant marriage, for some it meant divorce. . . .
What it all amounts to, I don't know. And I don't know
how much you can trust what anybody says about it, no
matter how accurate he may be at self-diagnosis and how
willing to state what he finds. But I'm sure that there was a
whole world of such motives operating somehow, in a
tangle behind the tangle. . . .

These comments on the tangled skein of motives
operating invisibly behind the show of events encourages a mistrust any historian feels towards his human

23

subjects. Perhaps they should also awaken a kindred mistrust for his own distorting mind and eye. If the men and women he interviews are guilessly contributing to the legend of the past, how can he be sure that he is not also the inadvertent falsifier dazzled by the mirage of the recent past and unable to divest himself of his own contemporaneity? The "objective" history shades into autobiography or merely adds another footnoted rumor to the historical romance of his times. Ideally, the historian should always be *in* history, so steeped and soaked in it that for short periods he loses his own identity. But of course he never can, or perhaps never should; for as Meinecke said, the historian "would thereby deprive himself of a source of perception." And what drives him to choose a man, a period, an event, is an inner necessity of which he may very likely be unaware.

When I wrote about the events of my own lifetime and of a selected group of people who flourished during this period, was I willy-nilly closer to these events imaginatively than I was, let us say, to the American Civil War? I dare say I was and that I should have been if I had never undertaken the study of the literary left and spent every day of my life plowing through the records of the "Great Rebellion." The sense, if not the meaning, of the recent past rubs off on a contemporary, even if he has walked through the tunnel of years in pitch blackness. In my case the tunnel was not completely dark, and my eyes were half-open. But in trying to resee these years through the eyes of other witnesses, the historian must cope with the tricks of memory and with unconscious falsifications and distortions—his own included. How faithful to the spoken and unspoken words are the notes for his interviews that help to determine his historical design? In the 1930's many writers looked at the world through a grille of bias. This ordered or "angled" perspective affected accounts of personal relationships, as well as history. Even during less passionate times, the astigmatic views of every recorder are corrected by built-in mechanical adjustments.

What gives the historian of contemporary events the sense that he is somehow face to face with reality is that the "facts" he purports to reveal are still close enough to their moment of birth to give him the illusion of their plasticity and liveness. *Rigor mortis* has not yet frozen them; the facts are not yet artifacts. Or to change the metaphor, recent facts retain for a time an afterglow. This is what the historian attempts to catch before the afterglow fades away. Yet it is only an afterglow, and the historian is very likely color-blind. As the contemporary ceases to be contemporary and drops into the past, compounded errors and paradoxes are discarded; blurred faces come into focus, and no eyewitness remains to say: "You're wrong. That wasn't the way they looked at all." Until these living testaments depart, the historian dares only to surmise. Depending upon people with fallible memories, trusting to the "reconsidered passion" of his informants, his attempts to reconstruct the recent past can be at best only experiments in model-building.

And yet these reflections on contemporary history must inevitably proliferate doubts about all history. The "inconsistencies and contradictions" the historian of the present detects in the living witnesses, as Alan Bullock reminds us, "are frequently bewildering, but the historian who hopes to escape from such conflicts of evidence by flying to the Sixteenth and Seventeenth centuries only deceives himself. For the history of the Sixteenth and Seventeenth centuries was once contemporary history—for the witnesses on whose evidence he has often to rely." In how many instances have the keys, the essential disclosures, been lost or unrevealed? And how much history, whether written by contemporaries or by historians centuries later, has been the work of misinformed people relying upon incomplete data?

Let us concede that the attempt to record the present can only result in a reasonably accurate facsimile. The historian's clumsy probings, nevertheless, may ultimately prove to be of greater usefulness than he suspects. Thanks to his occasional insights as well as blunders, his successors—less baffled by the "supple confusions" that obsessed him—will wander with more assurance through history's "contrived corridors" and "cunning passages" and possibly find an exit. In the meantime, the historian "trying (as Eva Reichmann has put it) to pierce through the tangle of present-day happenings towards an understanding of his own place in the maze" may share Henry Jame's delight in what he called "a palpable imaginable *visitable* past," a past close enough to be grasped, still unprotected by the "dignity" of history, and blending at once the strange and the familiar.

27

EDWARD LURIE

American Scholarship: A Subjective Interpretation
of Nineteenth-Century Cultural History

EDWARD LURIE

American Scholarship: A Subjective Interpretation of Nineteenth-Century Cultural History

I deliberately choose to call attention to the foregoing analysis as a "subjective interpretation" to emphasize, by tautology, what historians should exemplify as they weave tangled webs around the past and bequeath to later generations the hazards of historiography.* Since—by implication if not explication—in our hearts we know we are right, honesty and humility should compel us to hand down to our intellectual descendants our outgrown historiographical clothes in that philosophical spirit exemplified by John Dewey and Charles Beard that affirms the relativity of knowledge. Some of us would prefer to place faith in a Deity who, in the far future, would in His infinite Wisdom separate Truth from Falsehood, Right from Wrong, and make an ultimate pronounce-

* The generalizations and data advanced in this essay will be developed in my forthcoming study, *Cultural Transformation in Nineteenth Century America* (Oxford University Press). I am indebted to the John Simon Guggenheim Memorial Foundation for a Fellowship that made such research and writing possible in providing opportunity for study and writing. The literary and institutional aspects of the problems described herein will be analyzed in a collaborative volume with Daniel Aaron, *The Impact of the Civil War Upon American Culture* (Alfred A. Knopf, Inc.).

ment on the nature of the past settling once and for all the thorny problems of interpretation and reinterpretation. However, passing over what such an act would do to the business and the profession of historical and literary criticism, unless we ignore the nature of cultural change and choose to worship an ideal Platonic reality, or an equally ideal posterity such as that romanticized by Condorcet, it must be a central task of historical scholarship to demonstrate that evaluations of the past are necessarily relative, and only this epistemological condition is absolutely true.

Many have been tempted to embrace a reductionist view that history can be studied and its meaning laid bare through reliance upon processes and methods analogous to the laws of physical or biological science. In modern practice this impulse has been associated with a congruent urge to quantify historical data as if it were comprised of atoms, elements, or species, and thereby to applaud the viability of prediction regarding the future with the same certainty and confidence as that derived from knowledge that under similar conditions water will boil at a given temperature. To cite the variety of qualities of man, society, and nature that give to such efforts the character of artificial obstacles to the creative understanding of history and life would require too great a departure from the central themes of this analysis. At best, such efforts are misguided quests to escape from Daniel Aaron's dimly lit tunnel with positive faith that one's eyes will become fully open as a result. I suggest that Woodrow Wilson put the case well in warning against the fallaciousness of this reasoning from analogy when he wrote in regard to the dominance of science in late nineteenth-century American culture that

it is doing us a great disservice, working in us a certain degeneracy. . . . Its own masters have known its limitations. . . . But . . . all other men of all other studies have been set staring at their methods, imitating their ways of thought, ogling their results.[1]

It is the argument of this subjective interpretation of aspects of nineteenth-century cultural history that we know too little about the subject because of our failure to ask new questions about it. Such questions, asked with humility and phrased in the mode and manner that recognizes the subjectivity and relativity of knowledge and historical judgment should inspire innovative interpretations. Creative understanding of the past will hopefully be served more intelligently

1. "Princeton in the Nation's Service," *Forum*, XXII (December, 1896), quoted in Richard Hofstadter and F. Wilson Smith (eds.), *American Higher Education: A Documentary History* (Chicago, 1961), II, 692–93.

than before, because not only is it true that the facts do not speak for themselves, but it is also certain, as Dewey reaffirmed, that the questions asked of data determine the character of the answers and solutions that result. By persisting in holding outworn assumptions and attitudes toward this significant phase of national cultural history, the quest for understanding is axiomatically diminished by obstacles that block fresh insight. When Henry Sidgwick pointed out that we do not *solve* old questions but in fact get over them, he suggested a significant procedure for the process of historiographical creativity. Therefore, moderns will not be emancipated from the restrictive character of traditional approaches and old assumptions regarding nineteenth-century culture if, like flies, they continue as if trapped in the web of deception its contemporaries wove in describing it. To compound this sin, the web of past historiography has not only been accepted as "truth" but the process has been made less amenable to understanding by further scholarly emendations that merely repeat older notions. For historiography the result is comparable to Josiah Royce's complaint regarding informed knowledge of the Hegelian philosophy when he wrote that "almost everybody has forgotten what it means and has therefore come to accept it as true." [2]

2. Quoted in Bert James Loewenberg (ed.), *Charles Darwin: Evolution and Natural Selection* (Boston, 1959), p. 4.

The dead, and our own immediate predecessors in the writing of American cultural history, have consequently created a kind of memory hole regarding nineteenth-century life and thought—in this manner serving as comparable types to Mr. Aaron's "contemporaries"—and, because we have yet fully to heed the injunctions of Beard and Dewey, we are that much separated from creative understanding.

Two statements from the past at once underscore this condition and provide corrective insights to cope with it. The first, by Henry Adams, did much in emphasis and style to serve as a representation and exemplification of assumptions that constructed the fetters that bind us to a view of the past in which its commentators liked to believe. The second, which I will cite toward the close of this essay, is from George Santayana, and supplies the necessary philosophical and psychological techniques for placing the Adams statement in proper perspective.

The passage from Adams' *Education* is:

Had he been consulted, would he have cared to play the game at all, holding such cards as he held, and suspecting that the game was to be one which neither he nor any one else . . . knew the rules or the stakes? . . . Whether life was an honest game . . . or whether the cards were marked . . . he could not refuse to play his excellent hand. He could never make the . . . plea of irresponsibility. He accepted the situation . . . and . . . would do it again, the more readily for knowing the exact values. To his life . . . he was a consenting . . . party. Only with that understanding —as a consciously assenting member in full partnership with . . . society—had his education an interest to himself or to others. As it happened, he never got to the point of playing the game at all; he lost himself in the study of it, watching the errors of the players; but this is the only interest in the story, which otherwise has no moral and little interest.[3]

As Ernest Samuels has shown in his prescient untangling of the web Henry Adams wove, the assertive vigor of Adams' protest was in itself both a psychological and an empirical demonstration of his involvement in the game of late nineteenth- and early twentieth-century multiplicity. He not only played the game but, in a more important sense, he managed with an understanding of present and future so shrewd and acute that it exemplified commitment. That involvement comprised subtle yet powerful engagement yielding influential force in the elitist direction of politics, diplomacy, and culture. For Adams and his circle, power—to be effective— needed to be employed in discrete, long-viewing, often ironic fashion, so that superimposed rational persuasion would be the more lasting and effective. Such keen-minded decision-making by the men who gathered in the Adams house on H Street or in the rooms of Washington's Cosmos Club was the necessary

3. *The Education of Henry Adams* (Modern Library ed.; New York, 1931), p. 4.

counterforce to the dangers of late nineteenth-century populism. It was of no matter that such expansive economic or social democracy took the form of farmer protest, the muddying of legislative and presidential halls by General Grant and his political cronies of the nouveau stripe, or their analogues in the world of business and finance. This wasteful multiplicity of social and economic force required control and direction by men committed to a different view of progress. That advance was identifiable with the conservation of cultural and political power and value through the rational application of social resources, planned by cultivated men who understood the style of republican leadership. In the activist phase, that style, for Henry Adams, was revealed in his efforts to recount the virtues of the years of the early republic, the life of Albert Gallatin, and the artfully constructed mode of interpreting the deficiencies of his own lifetime and society in *Democracy* and the *Education*. It was essential to the Adams cultural style that he rarely allowed acknowledgements—by himself or by others—of his cultural influence, for such behavior would itself contradict a psychological tenet of the elitism he exemplified. Adams therefore took sober pleasure in publishing *Democracy* anonymously and circulating the *Education* to a select and limited group, and he secretly delighted in the effect he had

37

created. Adams' career and motives are ladened over and over again with ironies at once fascinating and maddening; but perhaps the supreme irony of all that may be attributed to him is the legacy this fine historian left to his colleagues of the future in their efforts to understand and untangle the history of those years whose character has so strongly borne the stamp Adams gave it. The understanding of the years of Adams' own lifetime (1838–1918) must go forward on two levels: an appreciation of the elitist drives that conditioned the cultural attitudes of men such as Clarence King, John Hay, Adams, and Henry Cabot Lodge, and, in significant counterpoint, with the open-minded spirit to emancipate historiographic judgment from the very obstacles placed upon it by the view such men held of their own era.

In 1913, Henry Cabot Lodge published *Early Memories,* the autobiographical account of his youth and growth to maturity and developing political awareness through formal and informal New England education. Its pages quite predictably documented the style and influence of Henry Adams upon the shaping of such men as Lodge, depicting in this way the social and intellectual manifestations of the mugwump persuasion. In this sense, the volume was a kind of preface to the *Education,* though far less didactic and

subtle. Upon reading it, Adams wrote his friend
deprecating such attributions of influence with the
words:

Looking on the whole affair from the outside . . . I could
rarely see which way to go, and was fantastically conscious
that others knew less than I, and were doing heaps of harm.
To this moment I am at a loss to know how I could have
done good. I cannot even say that in the actual situation I
see any clear path to it. . . . This attitude of mine I held
to be imbecile, and in effect I said so in my Education.
It deserves reprobation and scorn. . . . But! I still see
no more clearly what to do about it. Should I follow you?
I am willing enough, but just where do you stand? Shall
I follow Mr. W. J. Bryan? Good! but tell me, my pastor,
where to seek him![4]

In this same year, Adams read still another Brahmin
autobiography, Henry James's *Notes of a Son and
Brother*. His reaction was in the same vein. "Poor
Henry James thinks it all real," Adams intoned
derisively to Elizabeth Cameron, "and still lives in
that dreamy, stuffy Newport and Cambridge, with
papa James and Charles Norton and me! Yet, why!" [5]
Taking sharp issue with such deceptive fatalism,
James responded to Adams' words—reactions the
historian had probably communicated to the novelist

4. Adams to Lodge, October 18, 1913, in Harold Dean Cater
(comp.), *Henry Adams and His Friends* (Boston, 1947), p. 760.

as well—with the tones of a man at once admiring and made weary through bearing the impress of the Adams personalization of history:

Of course the past that was our lives is at the bottom of an abyss . . . of course, too, there's no use talking unless one particularly *wants* to. I still find my consciousness interesting. . . . Cultivate it *with* me dear Henry—that's what I hoped to make you do. . . . You see, I still, in presence of life (or what you deny to be such) have reactions—as many as possible—and the book I sent you is proof of them. It's, I suppose, because I am that queer monster, the artist, an obstinate finality, an inexhaustible sensibility.[6]

Adams' departure from stuffy old New England in 1877 had perhaps deprived him of that very *sensibility* that the Brahmin mind (even if it reflected upon America in Italian climes) epitomized in its talent for taking a long view of culture and history. If Adams believed, short-sightedly, that America had become a multiplicity of forces impervious to individual control or determination, he had done much from his new power base in Washington to create that energy-machine he seemed, on the surface, to despise. He enjoyed the sparkling image of purpose and power exemplified by a Clarence King who dashed off on great exploring expeditions, only stop-

5. Quoted in Ernest Samuels, *Henry Adams: The Major Phase* (Cambridge, Mass., 1964), pp. 550–51.

6. *Ibid.*, p. 551.

ping off at the capital now and then to gain large appropriations from Congress. He relished the soirees at the Cosmos Club, since that grouping of worldly individuals, led by Major John Wesley Powell, planned the direction of federal influence and appropriations in matters of science and related public policy. In the same mode and manner were the character of his relationships with such men of influence as John Hay and Cabot Lodge. Adams reveled in it all, especially after he could pronounce that thermodynamics and its American expositor, Josiah Willard Gibbs, had revealed that it was fruitless to presume to influence the course of universal energy dispersal. It became more fun to do so and then say that nothing had been, or could have been, done at all. Adams, then, contrived to oppose the newer, expansive power of the late nineteenth century with the means of established, traditional techniques identifiable with elitist ordering of society. His Adams forebears would have been properly appreciative of such an engagement with the world. But Adams' involvement was, of necessity, the kind of social relationship that perforce made him oppose the power of Grantism or *nouveau riche* manners with equally powerful self-conscious and self-selected aggregations of influence. It was this very character and manner of the elitist direction of culture that required Adams to play the role of the man-in-the-wings, who watched the errors of the players with increasing cynicism and pessimism. This duality of purpose and vision led him to strike poses and stances such as the one that earned James's rebuke. His attitude toward the history of his own life and times demanded an apparent loss of sensibility and dark pessimism, because that was the basic world view required by an individual who needed at once to appear disengaged all the while that he attempted to shape society and manners to the purposes of an elitist social order. But the net result was that Adams succeeded too well. He confused, and thereby convinced, many of his contemporaries regarding his essential cynical detachment. Still worse, his self-conscious parading of insensibility bequeathed to latter generations a view of his own world that, while psychologically significant to him, has been accepted at face value by his historian descendants.

Even on the basis of surface examination, it is obvious that the years Adams claimed to be infected with cultural vapidity lacked the materialistic spirit and Robber Baron style that would justify calling the period a gilded age, unfriendly to ideas, culture, and spirit. What is striking is that modern analysts have only rarely attempted to view the middle and latter decades of the nineteenth century through the device of different conceptualizations. Still less have they applied the more traditional canons of fact-gathering and "evidence" to dispel earlier misconceptions. Apparently, it is a perfectly viable procedure to produce new interpretations of such comfortable realms of being as economics, politics, and diplomacy; but the extension of the procedure, and even some of the data, of such discovery into the realm of ideas and culture is somehow disregarded. The result is that new insights are usually buried in the too often ignored modern work of the "literary" historian or the biographer, and the picture of these years remains essentially unchanged from that pressed upon us by a Henry Adams and adopted and adapted to the special cultural purposes of the 1920's and 1930's by such men as Vernon Louis Parrington or Matthew Josephson. Indeed, it is an irony of historiography that latter generations of analysts typical of a Jeffersonian and populist persuasion regarding the role of ideas and intellectuals in democratic society should adopt—for their own special purposes—the assumptions about cultural vapidity fashioned for them by a republican such as Henry Adams, whose preconceptions provided him with the strength to oppose both popular expansiveness and the oppressive dominance of the new political and economic corruption.

As the webs Henry Adams wove blinded him to sensibility, what essential ingredients of his world did he leave unchartered from his vantage points of Washington and the Pacific isles? It is noteworthy that in the very years Adams fashioned his deception upon himself, his society, and his successors, three of the most distinguished men of the mind of our cultural history lived lives parallel to Adams'. But, as distinct from the historian, the careers of Willard Gibbs, Charles Sanders Peirce, and George Santayana were spent largely in stuffy old New England, and, unlike that of Adams, theirs were lives of virtual isolation.

Santayana preferred the Harvard Yard and later, Italy, as appropriate environments from which to depict the assumptions and the fallacies of transcendentalism and pragmatism. In the case of Peirce, the contrast between him and his father was notable. A fairly distinguished astronomer and mathematician at Harvard, Benjamin Peirce was also a man deeply involved in the politics of young American science. He functioned as a guiding spirit within the councils of the "Order of Scientific Lazzaroni," that group of radical republicans of science and culture—spurred on by the drive of such new men of power as Alexander Dallas Bache and Louis Agassiz—who did much to influence higher education, professional association, and government in the years between 1850 and 1870. Significantly, this was an alliance that was national in scope; and as the cultural and psychological concept of union became more and more dominant, the Lazzaroni branched out from their early regional power bases in Albany, New Haven, Philadelphia, and Cambridge to center decision-making effort in Washington. Here, from the late 1840's through the turn of the century, such institutions as the Smithsonian, the National Academy of Sciences, and the United States Coast Survey became focal points of influence for them and their allies within the science establishment. That establishment needed political alliances and helpers, and found such support in men such as Henry Wilson, E. R. Hoar, Charles Sumner, and their later nineteenth-century compatriots of the mugwump mentality. In fact, one can trace direct connections between the Saturday Club of Boston in the immediate pre–Civil War years, the Lazzaroni of eastern centers whose influence extended through the 1870's, and the scientists and politicos of the Cosmos Club active in the years from the 1870's through the turn of the century. Of all the Lazzaroni, Agassiz, Bache, and Benjamin Peirce were by far the dominant figures, transforming, as it were, the elitist drives of the new professional science into modes that embraced political influence, economic alliances, and educational innovation. It is significant, too, that Bache and Peirce

45

each served as superintendents of the United States Coast Survey, employing this first national institution of intellectual activity as a power structure for their elitist drives and aspirations. Each man, in his own way, heralded and presaged the kind of society Henry Adams found at once so fascinating and so susceptible to the wise application of subtle influence and direction.

If father Peirce was a *prophetic* type, representing the full-blown form and style of elitist professionalism so prominent in national culture of the post–Civil War years, son Charles was in fact a *regressive* one. He was unable to cope with the institutional culture of the new Johns Hopkins University, and, for what were apparently temperamental, personal, and professional reasons, the younger Peirce did not gain a tenure appointment. Another ironic quality of post–Civil War culture is found in this condition, because Hopkins was an institution whose origin was made possible by the host of alliances between new men of academic power and economic influence so notable in the middle and later decades of the nineteenth century, affiliations that had been prefigured by the efforts of men such as Agassiz, Bache, and the elder Peirce, and were now carried to fruition by institutional academics like Andrew Dixon White and Daniel Coit Gilman of Johns Hopkins. Moreover, while the deprivation of institutional identity, status, and support was more a mark of honor to personality types such as the young Emerson or Thoreau, and could be abjured by the socially secure Henry Adams, its absence in the case of C. S. Peirce was an unhappy condition of life. The same, of course, was true for Thorstein Veblen and Randolph Bourne in subsequent years, men whose personal and intellectual radicalism compelled them to criticize and oppose institutionalism at the same time as they were fascinated by the study of its deleterious processes and dependent upon the economic and social status it offered. No single feature so distinguishes the social aspect of the life of the mind in the late nineteenth century than this almost axiomatic involvement of intellectuals within the mosaic of institutional culture in the governmental, private, and educational realms. One fortunate aspect of the fruits of elitist power drives was that C. S. Peirce was able to gain the modicum of a livelihood through what would now be termed consultant activity for the U. S. Coast Survey, thus following, albeit in much lower key, in the footsteps of his father. But the general fact of C. S. Peirce's intellectual and personal existence was that he lived the greater part of his life in virtual isolation, in a house in that very stuffy Newport that Henry Adams derided. Yet it was in such a place that

this singularly gifted man formulated the principles
of mathematical logic that dignified him as a philosopher of nature unsurpassed in the modern history of
his discipline. In the case of Peirce, then, the dynamo
—regardless of the penalties and obstacles resultant
from multiplicity and conformity—did not generate
sufficient gilt to stifle purposeful creative effort. In
such an instance, the condition of alienation—much
more than the contrived posture of an Adams—tells
us more about the dynamics of personal creativity in
a world supposedly unfriendly to the life of the mind.

But to turn to another example—directly in the
institutional mainstream—how account for the career
of Willard Gibbs, a man who had explained for
Adams' pleasure the workings of that infernal machine that seemed to negate, by metaphoric existence,
any possibility of individual accomplishment except
for those who toiled as its inspirers and later its
slaves. As thermodynamics was the central concept
underlying the dynamo, so then were the conceptualizations of Gibbs basic to the formulation and elaboration of these physical principles. Yet Gibbs was
a man who lived all his life in quiet contemplation
in quiet New Haven, unaffected by Lazzaroni or Robber Baron alike. While the fires of the great barbecue
roared on, and the Grants and Goulds trod Henry
Adams' wilderness road doing heaps of harm, Gibbs

48

worked steadily away, unknown even to most of his Yale colleagues. This intellectual, however, was able to conceptualize the elegant mathematical and physical principles underscoring the conservation of that very energy Adams preferred to interpret as being dissipated.[7] To this day, physicists have not fully explored nor appreciated the genius of Willard Gibbs, a man who never complained of the multiplicity he explained.

As the historian Adams misconstrued and misconducted his love affair with Gibbs, it is understandable from the viewpoint of sensibility that it remained for a poet to comprehend such genius, and encapsulate it in a superb word portrait. I refer to the biography of Gibbs by Muriel Rukeyser, a book inspired by that poet hearing a physical chemist speak eloquently of the grandeur of Gibbs' work.[8]

Henry James would certainly have applauded such an effort. But, from the "modern" view, how credit the competence of a poet to depict the life and work of a physicist? A biography, moreover, whose catalytic inspiration was a poem depicting Gibbs's intel-

7. For a recent interpretation of Adams' interpretation of thermodynamics, see Joseph Mindel, "Uses of Metaphor: Henry Adams on Science," *Journal of the History of Ideas*, XXVI (January-March, 1965), 89–102.

8. Muriel Rukeyser, *Willard Gibbs* (New York, 1942, and, in paper, 1964).

49

lect and the world it flowered in, while the work itself was distinguished by the interweaving of nineteenth-century imaginative poetry and literary art, with its analogue in the creative majesty of Gibbs's "poems" of physical transformation. And, as a footnote to Mr. Aaron's observations about the 1930's, this was a work by a poet who had written with the same passion and about the same subjects as had Kenneth Burke. Imagine the dismay of the science establishment that owed its very existence to Gibbs's eminence! It could not credit nor allow the Gibbs portrait to stand as the poet had painted it. The record had to be set straight, because, after all, only an atom can reconstruct the biography of physics. Hence an "official" biography was commissioned and published,[9] the Rukeyser biography relegated to relative obscurity (only of late has it received the true critical acclaim it deserves); and the tangle behind the tangle was still difficult to unravel because sensibility is less honored in our own time than in the consciousness of cultivated men such as Henry James.

Henry Adams, of course, was hardly insensitive to the intellectual and moral currents that flowed in and around his life. Like Cabot Lodge, he appreciated the influence of distinctive minds, and in the *Education* he

9. Lynde P. Wheeler, *Josiah Willard Gibbs* (rev. ed.; New Haven, 1952).

had dignified Louis Agassiz as the only teacher he had ever learned anything from in four wasted Harvard College years. Clearly, the twin themes of almost overblown adulation and equally overdrawn cynicism in this one observation are typical of Adams' ambivalence toward his world and its institutions. But, even granting the Agassiz evaluation as a sincere appraisal, had Adams pondered the poetic reflection of another Brahmin, James Russell Lowell, (words written as that long-viewing man tried to express his sense of loss at Agassiz' death) Adams' education in sensibility might have been enhanced. In Italy, when Lowell learned of the passing of this hero of nature study, he filled eleven pages of the *Atlantic Monthly* in anguished praise, ending his celebration with lines that consoled him as they should have educated Adams and us:

The beauty of his better self lives on
In minds he touched with fire, in many an eye
. . . .
In endless file shall loving scholars come
The glow of his transmitted touch to share,
And trace his features with an eye less dim
Than ours whose sense familiar wont makes numb.[10]

10. *Atlantic Monthly*, XXXIII (May, 1874), 596.

51

The less dim eye of the historian is what might hopefully have been expected of an Adams or his successors, and is that which Mr. Aaron seeks to encourage. But how perform this vital task if we take at face value the tangled web woven by contemporaries, selected by ourselves and our immediate predecessors as the dominant and honored judges of past cultural history? Such a task, I suggest, may be performed by two complementary methods: the seeking out of divergent and distinctive evidence; and, the motive behind this fresh quest being emancipation from the compounding of historiographic errors, such as taking simple refuge in aphorisms like the "gilded age" or "great barbecue" to describe the culture of an era whose vital intellectual character is as yet undescribed. To pursue this task with meaning requires the sensibility of the artist to the perceptions of culture and life in both past and present, interwoven with the ability of the experimental scientist to remain dispassionate and alienated from cultural assumptions.

This prescription may at first glance appear as a banal truism, but the virtue of seemingly simplistic clichés is that they often characterize viable method if they are followed as an avowed act of faith and not merely as convenient lip service in the cause of pedagogy or historiography. In attempting to carry this effort forward, I must confess that I am often tempted, in personal quests to unravel the tangled web spun by my predecessors, to wish I could take simple metaphoric refuge in the plot summary of *Moby-Dick* given by Rosalind Russell in the musical comedy *Wonderful Town* when she observed, "Well, its about this whale."

While I am tempted by the simplicity of the whale, I cannot forget his color or the motives of his pursuer. Consequently, I am in the psychological condition as that aptly, if crudely, portrayed in the plot and words of a typical Hollywood science-fiction thriller of recent vintage. In the movie, the heroine, Deborah, is placidly viewing the grounds of her palatial country estate when a mechanical monster suddenly arises from the lake and attempts to spirit her child away. Much later in the evening, when the monster has been subdued through the efforts of military technology, Deborah is sitting on the veranda mulling over the events of the day. Her brother, pipe in hand, greets her with the inquiry, "Why the brown study, Deborah?" To which our heroine replies with a pained smile, "It's nothing, Jim, really; *I just can't get that Monster out of my mind.*"

That is just the problem. Historians cannot get the monster created for them by Adams, Twain, Parrington, and Josephson out of their minds—and I cannot get out of mine the strong intuition that I can turn that monster into a good white whale given the opportunity to unweave the webs of historiography. What gives me the presumptive right to think I can set the record straight? Who can say? I would take sustenance from the sensibility of the Jamesian narrator cited by Mr. Aaron in believing that the lies I discover sometimes lay bare the truth. Yet I go somewhat further in affirming the viability of tentative certitude regarding the past. I am made at once bold and humble by recalling the tale of the three baseball umpires who were discussing how each determined whether a pitch was a ball or a strike. The first arbiter maintained, simply, "I call 'em as I see 'em." The second disagreed violently, affirming, "I call 'em *as they are.*" The third umpire listened with tolerance to his two colleagues and merely opined, "Listen, boys, *they're nothing until I call 'em.*"

If our third umpire had not read Hume or Beard or Dewey, his attitude certainly accorded with their view of the subjectivity of knowledge. The good Bishop Berkeley, like Juliana Bordereau of *The Aspern Papers*, would prefer to leave judgment in the keeping of the Deity, believing that the truth is God's, and is best left alone. But for those of us who cannot get the monster out of our minds, and know it's not just all about that whale, some *operational* means must be adopted to reinforce that act of faith Beard pleaded for as essential to the craft of the historian. There is a virtue in being *in* history; and yet involvement, as in the case of Adams, may obscure realization of why one chooses a subject or writes about it from a particular viewpoint, thus tangling the web even further.

I can offer an example from personal intellectual history that comprised being outside and inside the process of reconstructing the past as these phases came to perception when I wrote Louis Agassiz' biography. Bearing Lowell's injunction in mind, I tried to set about, with eyes less dim, to gain a "true" picture of the man and of his impact upon science and culture. My initial attitude was one of perplexity. Here was an individual who was "wrong" in certain aspects of science, notably his views on racial inferiority and organic evolution, and hence not a "winner" in the same sense that Santayana, whose conceptions were at variance with the dominant thought patterns of his day, was not. The tendency had been to count Agassiz out in the listing of "significant" and "influential" figures in our intellectual history, and write it from the viewpoint of those who made socially valuable or ideationally progressive movements possible, or else from the framework of those who impressed society that nothing of significance had happened at all, as in the case of the cultural taste-makers of the late nineteeth century. Yet I also knew that the scientific impact of Agassiz could not be reduced as one equivalent to merely a tale "about this whale" (even though there was a monstrous animal of this genre in the Harvard museum, there because Agassiz had allegedly stolen it from another naturalist).

How, then, to get involved in and familiar with the inner history? Actually, I began from the "outside" in this endeavor, because when I started work I knew little about contemporary "truth" in biological science, especially the bases for evolutionary natural history. As it turned out, this proved a most fortunate ignorance, since I was able to become absorbed in the pre-Darwinian concepts Agassiz held, unencumbered as it were by the "truth" of what came after him. Lowell's plea was not heeded at first, and for the better, because I could become sensitive to the intellectual world Agassiz cherished free from the inevitable bias that would have resulted had I been more "informed." One incidental result was that I came to appreciate the importance of examining erroneous concepts and ideas existing in opposition to dominant thought patterns as a highly valuable technique for analysis in cultural history. I thus also learned a good deal about the relativity of values and knowledge in the history of science in particular and the history of ideas in general.

Education in the outer history had to follow, however, and began, of necessity, through the medium of comparing Agassiz' outworn metaphysics and classical view of biology with the established, modern viewpoint. Yet this feat was accomplished with relative ease. What was less simple, by far, was the gaining of a picture of the whole man, both in terms of typical "evidence" and the employment of logical, inferential, and psychological insight, so necessary to the craft of biography. From studying Agassiz' ideas of nature, I came to appreciate that he held them passionately, and that to him the life of the mind, the spirit, and the fabric of human emotion were all interwoven. Ideas, I concluded, could not be analyzed independently of the men who held them and gave them a force and spirit in the special context of specific cultural realms. The internal, personal document was thus as important as the external public statement.

As I sought to construct this mosaic of the whole man, however, I encountered obstacles of an internal and external nature. At first, the more I found out about Agassiz' personality, with my eyes less dim, the more I came to dislike the strutting egocentrism,

57

the identification of his own values with what was right for all science and national culture. It was this pose that quite probably prompted Emerson to write,

I saw in the cars a broad-featured, unctuous man, fat and plenteous as some successful politician, and pretty soon divined it must be the foreign professor who has had so marked a success in all our social and scientific circles, having established unquestionable leadership in them all; and it was Agassiz.[11]

Yet this was also the man who had apparently impressed Henry Adams so favorably, and who was idolized by his worshipful public audiences, special students of science and cultivated laymen alike. Just ten years after Emerson penned his appraisal, the Concord sage joined Oliver Wendell Holmes, Longfellow, and Lowell in celebrating Agassiz' fiftieth birthday, heralding his service to New England with wine and poetry. If there was an admixture of awe and cyncism in Emerson's early appraisal, the birthday celebration of May, 1857, at the Saturday Club reflected the impact of a man who had become a true culture hero.

As New England's evaluation of Agassiz soared, mine changed, too, as did that of his contemporaries. In the end I saw him as a man whose ambition to domineer national science and culture was so over-

11. Quoted in Edward Waldo Emerson (ed.), *The Early Years of the Saturday Club* (Boston, 1918), p. 31.

riding that he felt no guilt or contradiction between private values and public purposes, because he *knew* he was right, and, I concluded, he was. But what was he right about?

He was certainly wrong on the fundamental scientific issue of the times, and here his dogmatism was offensive to colleagues like Asa Gray or William Barton Rogers, who had greeted him, when he arrived from Switzerland in 1846, as a hero of science and yet, little more than a decade later, regarded him as "a fraud, a humbug," because of his intellectual intransigence on the evolution question and his popular attacks on it. Who was the more correct, however— scientists such as Gray, or public intellects like Dr. Oliver Wendell Holmes who wrote Agassiz in 1863 in the midst of such scientific disputation that

I look with ever increasing admiration on the work you are performing for our civilization. . . . You have gained the heart of our purpose; you have taken hold of our understandings . . . and you are setting up a standard for them which will gradually lift us to its own level in aspiration if not in performance.[12]

Agassiz had most certainly changed, the society he had entered in 1846 was itself in a state of transformation, and I had changed along with my subject

12. Holmes to Agassiz, October 20, 1863, Agassiz Papers, Houghton Library, Harvard University. Used by permission of the Harvard College Library.

and his environment. To the living, then, the dead are in this sense hardly consistent, and those who judge them must realize the duality of being in themselves and in their subjects. If Mr. Aaron's living contemporaries back and file, block out events, and contradict each other, the same is true of my dead ones. These living dead are not really protected by the dignity of history, can never become artifacts, and the corpse does live on.

It lives in special and unique manner for the historian trying to breathe life into it because ancestors and archivists are always present, sometimes to assist the recreator with generosity and skill, but in other instances to impede his task through silence, myth-purveying, or simple lack of co-operation.[13] The mythology surrounding a distinctive individual more often than not obscures more than it reveals, except for the fact that a man with such images surrounding him in posterity must have been truly exceptional in his lifetime. That exceptional character is, of necessity, involved with the problem of ancestors and archivists. It was problem enough for such individuals to cope with a non–New Englander wanting to do a biography of Louis Agassiz. There were also descen-

13. On the subject of archival research in American science, see Edward Lurie, "Some Observations on Research in Nineteenth-Century American Science," *Isis*, LIII (1962), 20–32.

dants, with personal papers under their control; and while the going was generally neither pleasant nor terribly difficult, there were times when I wondered whether the obstacles placed in my path would ever permit the task to be completed as it needed to be done. Even distinguished administrators of research establishments, as eager as they were to aid intellectual progress, had of necessity to consider what penalties might result from the displeasing of ancestors. After some years, and invitations into homes for the passing of muster, the temporarily disabling familial situation was overcome, and I do not think that congenial acceptance into New England parlors affected my judgment of Agassiz one way or the other. What did confuse me for a good while were the remembrances of individuals of diverse occupations and stations in life who knew that only they "remembered" some wonderful "Agassiz story" I should have to write up. For example: He *did* steal that monstrous whale. He did not. (Oh, were it all that simple!) He would not accept a Harvard professorship unless the college president had provided a house for his mistress. He had been the teacher of every American scientist from Rafinesque down to men of the early twentieth century (he lived from 1846 to 1873 in America). And on and on it went. I got the whale and mistress stories cleared up (he had been without sin in each case), but such mythology points up the vitality of the so-called dead past.

I learned something more from studying Agassiz' life that came as a revelation and cast a new light for me on the cultural history of the years of Henry Adams' lifetime. When I had previously debated with myself whether a Gray or a Holmes had been correct in their estimate of Agassiz' worth, it became clear that I had considered the question in either-or terms so that, as in the current division between "scholar" and "administrator" or "popularizer" I, and many of my colleagues, had been guilty of a historiographic misconception of rather enormous proportion.

Perhaps because America could boast of so few individuals who advanced the life of the mind, and also because its historians have evidenced a consistent insecurity regarding the intellectual "achievements" of Europe constrasted to native accomplishment, we have tended to confer cultural status to those who "contributed" to intellectual history. Moreover, we adopted a congruent attitude in our estimate of the scholar that held that if he did not produce correct, socially useful, or psychologically comfortable interpretations, he was damned to the perdition of repute as a popularizer or, still worse, administrator of knowledge. Pause for a moment and reflect as to your instinctive reaction to the terms "technology," "univer-

sity president," "robber baron," and "dynamo," and
I think my point is apparent. You just can't get that
monster out of your minds, and this psychological
inhibition is the more restrictive in gaining a new
understanding of the relationships between intellectuals and society in the nineteenth century.

The artificiality of the traditional view became
more striking as I reflected on the meaning of Agassiz'
later career, from the 1850's until his death. Such
false distinctions seemed oppressive in the quest for
understanding that special situation and, more generally, the character of cultural history from the
1830's through the turn of the century.

In the most creative period of his American career,
Agassiz was truly a public man. He established, organized, and rationalized aspects of culture in a fashion
and to a degree that he and others of similar persuasion made possible the preconditions for the profes-
sionalizing of knowledge and the elitist conservation
of cultural energy. Adams did not learn this style of
life from Agassiz, but it is indisputable that the same
impulse was writ large in the social attitudes of each
man. The process of rationalization—begun by such
men as the scientific Lazzaroni—resulted in the building of lasting institutions that not only did much to
shape the configurations of our own world but also
provided Agassiz and his successors with the financ-

ing, the cultural status, and the social framework to pursue the advancement of knowledge under conditions such men as John Quincy Adams had pleaded with his society to provide.

Who is to judge, then, that an Agassiz or a Gilman or a Charles William Eliot, who dedicated their lives to the building of institutions to house the intellect of the Jameses, the Santayanas, or the Gibbses, was less an "intellectual" than other types? If we define intellectual history solely in terms of men who won or made things happen of a character that can be quantified or deemed immediately influential from the social aspect, then it might actually appear that the record of the late nineteenth century is indeed a rather barren one. (Historians of "social thought" thus wait patiently until the curtain rises again and reveals the good Goddess of twentieth-century reform, whose precepts can be hashed over again and again as is the historiographic fate of Jacksonian reform or antislavery prior to those movements being swallowed up in the great barbecue). If it is understood, however, that the building and administering of institutions of intellect is just as creative an occupation as the study of systematic botany, then we come part of the way, at least, to unraveling the tangle behind the tangle.

Yet as the web becomes somewhat more understandable, unconsciously we do not like what we may

see with eyes wide open, and would really prefer to
take refuge in the comfortable symbol of the gilded
age and affirm it was really just about this whale after
all. Why? Because the evidence of the cultural history of the late nineteenth century points to the ce-
menting of alliances between public men of intellectual and academic power with analogous types from
the world of business and finance. This synthesis en-
abled academic men to fashion the power for the
operations of a cultural elite that nationalized and
rationalized much of American social existence. This
generalization requires elaboration and much testing,
but the general validity of it is apparent in the activities of such men as Cornell, Harper, Gilman,
White, and Eliot. Of course, a self-selection process
was underway within each personality grouping; men
of wealth chose men of academe most congenial to
their outlook and interests, while men of the academic
elite preferred to deal with long-viewing, far-sighted
benefactors of the sort typified by a John Amory
Lowell or an Abbott Lawrence in the prehistory of the
process of cultural superimposition. Types such as a
Henry Adams could take proper pleasure in decimat-
ing the image of the crude robber baron, but, if manners and style were conformable to the older values,
admission into the club was safely assured. Departing
from the realm of metaphor, one needs only examine

the membership and social history of such aggregations as the Cosmos Club, the Century Club, and the Saturday Club to discover a direct manifestation of such elitist alliances.

Hence we are forced to face up to the cultural fact that such types of personality as White, Cornell, Gilman, Jordan, Rockefeller, and Leland Stanford lived in rather close and comfortable harmony in creating new conditions of society and scholarship. Bear in mind that I make no evaluation that applauds such relationships. But they did exist, and the host of memoirs of such men as White, Eliot, Powell, F. W. Putnam, G. Stanley Hall, and Charles Eliot Norton provide ample evidence in this respect. So, too, do the analyses of Veblen and Beard, men caught up in the pressures and the culture of the new environment, and thus able to depict its forms and manners.

I should like to offer some tentative explanations as to why—given this quality of late nineteenth-century culture—we have come to prefer the self-conscious tangling of the web identifiable with Henry Adams or the simple banalities of his historian successors as "causative" tendencies defining this period. I think it plain that historians have become too obsessed with the study of populism in its expansive pre–Civil War aspects and its compulsive post-bellum and progressivist phases. We have become less able to realize that there existed in Adams' lifetime a republican, nationalist philosophy of culture that, in its pre–Civil War aspects, witnessed the shaping of notable alliances between intellectuals, politicians, and men of economic power. Such activities set the stage for the cultural nationalism typical of Civil War and late nineteenth-century America. Some of the cast of characters in this association of intellect and elitism remained constant throughout the period, while, in other instances, a Benjamin Peirce or an Alexander Dallas Bache was succeeded by a Charles William Eliot or John Wesley Powell, while a John Amory Lowell or Francis Calley Gray had as his latter counterpart a John D. Rockefeller or a Leland Stanford. Moreover, a notable type of individual was the man who acted as an intermediary between men of academic power and men of economic influence, and the activities of a Samuel Atkins Eliot before the war, or a Frederick T. Gates in the more modern period, are typical of such transmission belts and personal linkages between men of different worlds but of the same cultural persuasion. The impulse and style comprising such conservation and rationalization of culture was constant throughout the entire period; but its force and effective activity increased in direct proportion to the rather rapid rise to prominence of types of men whose values and personality were spe-

67

cially suited to such enterprise, efforts that grew with the increasing availability of large-scale financial support for institutional development. Most individuals of this kind considered populism in its political, economic, or social forms to be an expansive and consequently wasteful utilization of social energy. Henry Adams' need to delineate and attempt to control the multiplicity and force he associated with the symbol of the dynamo reflected this viewpoint. Such men were in no sense blind conservatives opposed to cultural progress; it was typical of the Brahmin mind and its latter mugwump attitude—as expressed by such men as Edwin P. Whipple and George William Curtis—that they served in the vanguard of the advancement of knowledge and culture through the inspiration of institutions beneficial to the life of the mind, to the same degree as a man of George Ticknor's persuasion had done in the Boston of an earlier era.[14] But progress, to be lasting and permanent, required the planned, ordered, rational control of cultural resources, and was hence identifiable with the intelligent conservation of energy and its wise direction into the most valuable and necessary enter-

14. See, for example, George William Curtis, *Orations and Addresses* (New York, 1894), especially chaps. xi and xiii, and Edwin P. Whipple, "Shoddy," in his *Success and Its Conditions* (Boston, 1871), chap. xviii.

prises, such as the new private universities or the new federal science establishments. It is of high interest, for example, that men such as Henry Adams, John Wesley Powell, and Theodore Roosevelt—taking their psychological substance from the current vogue of physics and biology—were all passionately dedicated to one idea and conceptualization. This construct was the notion of *conservation*, which had different procedural but similar substantive meaning for individuals such as these. It was as if the ideational appeal of thermodynamics had been syncretized with the analogous ordering of nature identifiable with the theory of organic evolution, so that J. Willard Gibbs and Charles Darwin had supplied thoughtful American men of intellect with a philosophy of natural process that, while grounded upon the concept of transformation in organic and inorganic creation, provided, at the same time, a supportive analogy to a social and political value system that affirmed the virtue of orderliness and efficiency. Viewed in this light, relationships between concepts of nature and theories of society appear to be much more useful tools for analysis and understanding than reliance upon outworn and relatively superficial generalizations regarding the influence of "Darwinism" in its reformist or conservative political and

69

economic applications. In fact, Henry Adams illustrated just this congruence between conservation and order in science, politics, and culture in the pages of the *Education* that were devoted to reflections on evolution and thermodynamics.

In terms of historiography, I am not insisting that modern analysts consign attention to the spirit of populism to the rubbish heap of outmoded points of departure or intellectual orientation. I am suggesting that in our preference for such a simple old whale, we may well have left unexplored a central thread in cultural history. I suspect, also, that there are psychological explanations—residing in the emotional conditioning of historians active since the 1930's— that have served as obstacles to such fresh analysis. This intellectual failure is the result, perhaps, of past and current ambivalence on the part of academics and popular writers to the world of organizations, foundations, and institutionalism. The result is a duality of values expressed as a fascination, absorption, and positive affirmation in accepting the values of such contemporary forms of academic style, while the converse mentality expresses itself in an unconscious or sometimes violently articulate and vitriolic deprecation of establishment psychology in its current forms. In the attempt to retain the cake of independence and respectability and, at the same

time, to seek for the outward signs of status and
approval conferred by elitist symbols of distinction,
the modern academic, especially in non-scientific
areas, is often an individual torn by conflicting
drives and emotions that make him both unhappy
with his lot in life and hopefully eager to do something to control and master the forces that seem to
direct him, helplessly, ever onward to seek signs of
prestige and status. On the modern and conscious level
he vents his frustration against institutionalism by
railing against committees, organizations, university
presidents, and the all-embracing evil of "administration," effectively helping to widen a Snow-like gap
between men of the mind and men devoted to the
administration of knowledge. It is as if he was sustained at once by the values of a Randolph Bourne,
but propelled forward by the fascination of a Veblen
with technological efficiency, or the fond hope that
John Dewey was really correct and that the modern
man of the mind can control the social forces of his
environment by accepting their assumptions, joining
the club as it were, and turning the monetary and
ego-supporting guns of the intellectual establishment
to purposes that he and fellow right-thinking colleagues deem to be ideally valuable. This is not the
place to speculate on the effects of such psychological
ambivalence or protestations of self-rectitude upon

71

the intellectual as free or alienated social critic. Academics suffering from this condition have failed to face up to the reality that some of the selfsame teachers and intellectual forefathers they cherish did much to foster the very conditions of social existence that they at once despise and accept because they feel either powerless to control them or emboldened with the notion that right reason will triumph in good Jeffersonian fashion if good men are charged with the implementation of power. Hence the love affair with Henry Adams, because he lived through an earlier time of the same character, evaluated it in pejorative terms (albeit for his own purposes), and the cultural history of that time remains largely misconceived, so that the monster is still very much in the academic mind.

It was driven out for me by an ultimate appreciation of what a personality such as Agassiz could create—outside himself—for the rationalization and progress of cultivated society. That awareness came as I read a series of letters between the Harvard naturalist and Senator Charles Sumner written in the spring and summer of 1864. Agassiz, Peirce, Bache, and other Lazzaroni had founded the National Academy of Sciences the year before, perhaps the supreme example of the early period in the effort to rationalize the life of the mind. "I had hoped to

receive two good lists for our other two academies,"
wrote Sumner, who had made the same request of
Emerson and had received sympathetic support from
the still vital membership of the Saturday Club.
"Beset by engagements as I am, how can I prepare
such lists? You are among our lettered men. Talk
with them and help me. Send me two complete lists,
one for literature, the other for social science."
Agassiz replied to this appeal with the words, "With
a whale, 47 feet long upon my hands [you see?]
. . . I have not been able to do much towards answer-
ing your questions, though I have been thinking of
the matter all the time." He went on to list the full
membership of two groups to be sponsored by the
national government and established as formal academies, one of letters, the other of social science.
It is understandable and quite predictable that of the
total of thirty-seven names agreed upon by Agassiz
and Sumner, all can be traced to affiliations with the
Lazzaroni, the *Atlantic Monthly*, the Saturday Club,
or similar elitist aggregations in Washington, New
York, and Philadelphia, with the preponderance of
established intellectual virtue centered in Cambridge,
Boston and Newport.[15] The fact that the proposed

15. Sumner to Agassiz, May 11, 1864, Agassiz to Sumner, June
15, 1864, Agassiz Papers, Houghton Library, Harvard University.
Used by permission of the Harvard College Library. See also Ralph
Rusk (ed.) *Letters of Ralph Waldo Emerson* (New York, 1939),
V, 392–97.

academies failed to receive congressional charters is irrelevant to the central significance of this effort, the manner in which elitism and the urge to conserve and order cultural activity became more and more a central feature of existence first in the scientific and then in the social scientific and humanistic realms. The late nineteenth-century history of higher education and associational activity in non-scientific areas of *academia* provides still additional and more preponderant evidence substantiating the character of such transformation.

In the effort to trace the specific form and substance of this notable phase of cultural history, the analyst is fettered by more than ordinary problems of method, evidence, and the evaluation of data. Since men engaged in nefarious practices do not always write them down, a considerable portion of what might normally be considered "evidence" in traditional realms of historical scholarship resides, in this area, in the realm of logical, inferential, and psychological interpretation. But such data—while hardly as "demonstrable" as the evidence of voting behavior or the views contained in Congressional debates—is nevertheless equally valid, to the extent that the interpreter approaches the material at hand with insight, maturity, and the intellectual sophistication to see his task as one of synthesizing aspects of information that might on the surface appear to be unnoticed bits and pieces of associational alliances, interlocking directorates of power, and the sometimes revealing words and phrases of men willing to confide to paper their inner motivations and aspirations. Such a task must be viewed as one in which "conclusions" and "generalizations" are at best partial and tentative, and its quality is such that the historian must never yield to the attitude of mind typified by the dogmatism of the opposed persuasian that by definition rules out the life of mind as nearly nonexistent or at least highly insignificant in these years.

Louis Agassiz never wrote an autobiography—nor did many of his fellows. Henry Adams did perform such a cultural service, but how read his effort as it needs to be read, and how read what men of elitist persuasions said of themselves or liked to believe about themselves with a sensibility they may not have possessed? In following the command of James Russell Lowell, and the quest of Mr. Aaron, it is worthy of note that in the very year Adams wrote his *Education*, 1906, a method and philosophy for such historical interpretation was offered by George Santayana. In *The Life of Reason*, Santayana observed, with a sensitivity and perception he was not supposed to show at the end of the gilded age and near the beginnings of the period of dynamic reform,

75

In the natural history of man such interpretation into mental terms . . . is . . . legitimate because language allows people, perhaps before their feelings are long past, to describe them in terms which . . . refer directly to mental experience. The sign's familiarity, to be sure, often hides . . . a great vagueness and unseizableness in the facts; yet a beginning in defining . . . the mental phase of natural situations has been made in those small autobiographies which introspective writers sometimes compose. . . . *What a man under special conditions may say he feels or thinks adds a constituent phase to his natural history;* . . . were these reports exact and extended enough, it would become possible to enumerate the precise sensations and ideas which accompany every . . . social situation.

This advantage, however, is the source of that confusion and sophistry which distinguish the biology of man from the rest of physics. *Attention is there arrested at the mental term, in forgetfulness of the situation which gave it warrant, and an invisible world, composed of these imagined experiences, begins to stalk behind nature . . . independently.* This metaphysical dream . . . [has] two stages: the systematic one, which is called idealism, and an incidental one which pervades ordinary psychology, in so far as mental facts are uprooted from their basis and deprived of their . . . spiritual character, in order to be made elements in a dynamic scheme. *This battle of feelings . . . might be called a primitive materialism . . . for forms and realizations are taken . . . for substantial elements, and are made to figure either as a part or as the whole of the world's matter* [italics supplied].[16]

It was too bad, in a way, that Henry Adams had left

16. *The Life of Reason,* a one-volume edition revised by the author in collaboration with Daniel Cory (New York, 1953), p. 421.

stuffy old Cambridge. For it would seem that Santayana had read the *Education,* and had had a quiet discussion about it with Henry James, or, perhaps, with the ghost of papa James.

If the cultural pessimism of an Adams or a Twain was made by them and is contrived by us to figure as the world's subject matter, it is plain that we must, as Santayana urged, read such documents with great care, realizing the battle of feelings they represented and the transistory nature of their recapitulation of the past or the present.

To drive the monster from our minds with at least temporary conviction, still another realization must enter the consciousness of the historian. That is that if the late nineteenth century was a period unfriendly to the life of the mind, then it would seem that bigger great barbecues are prime conditions for the progress of intellectual history. In the same era when the United States is alleged to have been infected by an overriding materialism, and the dynamos whirred on uncontrollably, is it not more than curious that this was also a period of highly significant achievement in the realms of philosophy, literature, science, and architecture? As regards philosophy, is it not noteworthy that, in the work of Santayana, Royce, and their followers, this period witnessed a vital time in the history of American idealism? Clearly, the alleged material culture of the gilded age failed to influence some of its major philosophical figures. In more catholic interpretation, when one notes that these were years that witnessed the work of Dewey in his formative period, of Royce, of Chauncey Wright, and of Lester Ward, I suggest we need a new definition of the American Renaissance. If history and the social sciences are considered, surely Woodrow Wilson, Frederick Jackson Turner, Veblen, E. A. Ross, Richard T. Ely, Simon Patten, G. Stanley Hall, and even Henry Adams himself seemed to survive the errors being made by the players of the game. I make no claim to special competence in literary history or analysis, but it seems self-evident that a period that witnessed the work of such men as Howells, Henry James, Stephen Crane, and a host of other distinguished writers and poets was not the kind of belletristic blank that would seem a necessary condition to the historiographic assumption regarding lack of cultural vitality. Obviously, the distinct and distinguished history of American architecture speaks for itself in this period; and while it is intellectually unprofitable to evaluate it in terms of what came before or that which followed, it is the case that the concrete symbolization of American multiplicity was testimony on still another level to the creative "achievements" of these years. Finally, when the

78

scientific work of such men as Gibbs, Remsen, New-comb, Bell, Langley, Alex Agassiz, Putnam, Powell, Boas, and a host of other equally notable figures in the history of the natural and physical sciences is noted, this era must be marked as one of the richest ones in the history of those disciplines.

From this limited evidence, even if we accept the essentially false dichotomy between the creative or-ganizer and the creative "solitary" intellectual, it is plain that the Washington of the Cosmos Club, the New Haven of the Sheffield Scientific School, the America of the Roman air, or the Harvard Yard of the Golden Age all contained inhabitants and intellec-tual elements of high quality. Hence, the men asso-ciated with this period did not suffer from the stifling fetters that historians of the 1930's—employing in-complete evidence and motivated by emotional bias —defined as the basic character of the life of the mind and its surrounding cultural context. Lest it appear that I am making Henry Adams or Twain the villains of this analysis, I want to make it plain that, as Santayana's injunction implied, we, with eyes that should be far less dim, are much more guilty than our predecessors of the past. In fact, as Royce put it, we know so little about the actual character of cultural and intellectual history in these years that we have come to accept as true the pejorative notions our predecessors handed down to us, thereby further tangling the web.

It should be self-evident that there are different and more imaginative ways of looking at the middle and late decades of the nineteenth century than we have yet given ourselves the pleasure of doing, through a failure to exercise inexhaustible and un-committed sensibility. This was, after all, a world large enough to contain the elitist drives of a Powell, an Adams, a King, or a Gilman; the perceptive analytic alienation identifiable with Santayana; the philosophical and psychological achievements of Wil-liam James, and the literary genius of Henry James. In sum, I underscore Henry James's plea to Henry Adams that historians should cultivate the study of these times with as many reactions as possible, guided by the spirit exemplified in Louis Agassiz' philosophy of education when he told Americans to study nature and not rely merely on books, and that "a physical fact is as sacred as a moral principle." [17]

17. Recent scholarship has demonstrated a new concern with advancing divergent interpretations of American culture in the years under discussion. See, for example, H. Wayne Morgan (ed.), *The Gilded Age: A Reappraisal* (Syracuse, 1963); David T. Gil-christ and W. David Lewis (eds.), *Economic Change in the Civil War Era* (Greenville, Delaware, 1965); and Edward Lurie, "Nine-teenth-Century American Science: Insights from Four Manuscripts," *Rockefeller Institute Review* (January-February, 1964), pp. 11–19, and Lurie, "Science in American Thought," *Journal of World History,* VIII (April, 1965), 638–65.

STOW PERSONS

The Origins of the Gentry

STOW PERSONS

The Origins of the Gentry

When the English liberal writer Harriet Martineau recounted her travels in the United States in 1834 and 1835, she referred frequently to the "gentlemen" and "ladies" whom she had met. It is clear that to her these gentry folk constituted an important social class. They were people of cultivated manners, refined speech, distinctive clothing, and engaged in kinds of activity appropriate to their education and social position. She carefully distinguished them from "aristocrats," whom she regarded as an anomaly in a democratic republic. The gentry were a highly desirable class, unostentatious in manner, democratic in sympathies, and dedicated to the cultivation of learning and refinement. They were, of course, the American counterpart of the British class to which Miss Martineau herself belonged; they were the people to whom she brought her letters of introduction and under whose auspices she was introduced to American society.[1]

1. *Society in America* (3 vols.; 2nd ed.; London, 1837), I, 64; III, 92–96. Throughout this paper I refer to the gentry as a "class," although I am aware that the usage may seem of doubtful validity to some readers. In conventional usage class is conceived in terms of stratification on a vertical scale as measured by economic and

The early nineteenth century was the golden age of this gentry class. "What fact more conspicuous in modern history," Emerson demanded to know, "than the creation of the gentleman?" The word rattled in his ear like a flourish of trumpets. "The gentleman is a man of truth, lord of his own actions, and expressing that lordship in his behavior, not in any manner dependent and servile either on persons, or opinions, or possessions." Collectively, the gentry were a "self-constituted aristocracy of the best" that perpetuated itself without written law or usage, appropriating beauty or talent wherever they appeared. The gentleman was the ultimate embodiment of Emerson's great principles of individualism and self-reliance.[2] Likewise, when Jefferson spoke of a natural aristocracy of virtue and talent as distinguished from an artificial

related indexes. In fact, however, the social conditions of fluidity and mobility that have intrigued observers of the American scene since the beginning of the nineteenth century have seriously compromised a word better suited to the older regimes of Europe. Yet it is the consensus of historians that the word "class" is too useful to abandon, as a cursory inspection of a random sample of historical works will attest. Its persisting use represents a triumph of convenience over precision. My designation of the gentry as a class is meant to suggest a widely diffused social group of appreciable size unified externally by the visible symbols of gentility and internally by preoccupation with distinctive problems and standards. While it is also apparent that the gentry occupied a discernible place in the stratification system, as indicated in section 2 of this paper, that aspect of the history of the class is of lesser concern for the moment than its intellectual history.

2. "Manners," *Essays, Second Series,* in *Works* (4 vols. in 1; New York, n.d.), I, 316–18.

aristocracy of birth and wealth, he was defining his own conception of a gentry class.

James Fenimore Cooper had much to say about the indispensable role of the gentry in a democratic society. Addressing himself to Europeans in his *Notions of the Americans*,[3] Cooper praised the American gentry for their simplicity of deportment and for their comparative obliviousness to money as the criterion of social standing. He defined the gentleman as "one elevated above the mass of society by his birth, manners, attainments, character and social condition." He believed it possible in a democratic society to be a gentleman without distinguished family antecedents, and he was emphatic that money was not a necessary ingredient of gentility. It was certainly true that a person born in a gentry family and nurtured in the standards of the class enjoyed a great advantage; but, fortunately, simplicity was the first great quality of a gentleman, and if the aspirant could reach only this he would have something well-worth-while.[4]

The principal avenue of access to the gentry for those not born in gentry families was provided by formal educational opportunities. There were innumerable instances of poor farm or city boys who

3. *Notions of the Americans: Picked Up by a Travelling Bachelor* (2 vols.; London, 1828), I, 204–9.
4. *The American Democrat* (New York, 1931), pp. 84–91.

showed an aptitude for schooling, managed to go to college, and thus acquired the skills and interests that admitted them to the world of the gentry. The educational mode of access had much to do with fixing the professional, literary, and almost classical tone of the class. Even in Boston, where according to common impression the gentry were an exclusive lot, admission to the class was open to men and women of talent regardless of background. The historians John Gorham Palfrey and Jared Sparks, for instance, both rose from poverty and obscurity to secure positions of gentry leadership. Even without formal education, the standards of gentility were readily available for emulation. Emerson observed that all of English fiction from Sidney to Scott reflected the character of the gentleman. In addition to the memorable portraits of ladies and gentlemen in Fielding, Addison, and Jane Austen, there were the didactic essays on gentility by Chesterfield and Chatham available in numerous American as well as British editions.

A prominent place in gentry ranks was held by professionals: doctors, lawyers and judges, the educated clergy, and teachers. There were also artists, writers, journalists, editors, and publishers. But many business men, merchants, bankers, engineers, and civil servants had firmly established gentry status. Although a traditional stereotype of the gentleman identified him as a man of leisure, this was not generally the case with the American gentleman. He need not be a man of wealth, although he was expected to command comfortably spacious housing and servants. Cooper in one of his more sanguine moods was able to persuade himself that American institutions and opinions assigned no artificial importance to wealth! [5] In any event, the gentry themselves generally judged one another not by the pocketbook but by the ideal standards of gentility.

The visible symbols of gentility furnished the overt indications of the status of the gentry as a class; the inner life of the class was dedicated to the fostering and advancement of high culture. The nineteenth-century gentry was the culture-bearing class, and so long as it survived as a class, it was able to impart to American cultural and intellectual life distinctive qualities derived from the commitment to gentility. The gentry constituted a kind of cultural "establishment." Through substantial control of such institutions as colleges and schools, learned academies and reviews, publishing houses, and the educated pulpit, it was able to place its stamp upon the products of cultural activity. The disciplined and cautious tone of gentry culture is reflected in the remark of Longfellow that "all literature, as well as all art, is the result of culture and intellectual refinement."

5. *Notions*, II, 416–21.

There was a strong tendency among gentlemen to idealize themselves and their social role. Edward Everett declared that the word "gentleman" was properly used only with reference to a person of character, integrity, and intelligence. As a class, the gentry was dedicated to the perpetuation of the best things in life, and its members expected that society would gladly elevate them to the honored position merited by their virtue and talent.

II

Historians have generally overlooked the gentry as a distinct social class; they have submerged it in a loosely defined upper class or "aristocracy." [6] But many contemporary observers distinguished carefully between gentry and the social-economic elite; and for a proper understanding of the historical role of the gentry, it is essential to do this. The social-economic elite organized themselves as Fashionable Society, and because they also patronized the outward conventions of gentility and thought of themselves as ladies and gentlemen, it is not surprising that the distinction

6. An exception that should be noted is Edwin Cady, *The Gentleman in America* (Syracuse, 1949). Cady's book, however, is principally a literary, rather than a social, history. For a comprehensive study of the idea of gentility in Western culture, see Esmé Wingfield-Stratford, *The Making of a Gentleman* (London, 1938).

between the two classes has been commonly over-looked.[7]

Harriet Martineau not only noted the existence of the two groups but she also pointed to the significant ideological fact that in the 1830's the aristocracy, which congregated at the fashionable watering places, were distinctly antidemocratic in outlook, while the gentry were firmly committed to the democratization of American society.[8] Emerson undertook to explain the dynamic relationship between the two classes. Manners, he said, originate spontaneously in the social intercourse among gentlemen. Once fixed by usage, these manners acquire prestige and become the badge of social distinction. Thus fashion grows up. For Emerson, fashionable society was the hard shell secreted by the living organism of the gentry. Fashion, he said, is virtue gone to seed—a kind of posthumous honor. Fashionable society was composed

7. Social histories of the United States invariably recognize and describe the social life of the economic elite. For a typical treatment, see Dixon Wecter, *The Saga of American Society* (New York, 1937). Writing in the 1830's, Francis J. Grund referred to the fashionable "coteries" of wealthy families to be found in the seaboard cities. This term was well chosen to designate the relatively small and clublike groups united by congenial traits that constituted the fashionable society of that day (*American Quarterly Review,* XXII [1837], 427).

8. *Op. cit.,* III, 92–96. Francis J. Grund in *Aristocracy in America* (New York, 1959 [originally published, 1839]) confirmed Miss Martineau's impressions of the antirepublicanism of the elite.

of the children of the great; it was funded talent; and, inevitably, Emerson spoke slightingly of the polished manners of the "dress-circles" where they "put all on stilts." [9] Cooper made a similar distinction between what he called "the great vulgar world" and the "great *respectable* world." The former produced fashion, and the latter, something far more valuable and enduring.[10]

More circumstantial accounts of this social distinction were furnished by other literary folk whose recollections extended back to the time in the mid-nineteenth century when the two classes played significantly different roles. Reminiscing about her childhood in a socially distinguished elite family in New York, Edith Wharton recalled that although members of the family had genuine intellectual interests, they were fearful of intellectuals in the flesh. Irving, Fitz-Greene Halleck, and Longfellow might be acknowledged as gentlemen; but most contemporary writers, including Poe and Melville, were unknown to polite society, while Harriet Beecher Stowe was despised as being "common." It was a regrettable fact, Mrs. Wharton concluded, that in provincial societies gentry and elite should look askance at each other. The scholars, artists, and men of letters stubbornly shut themselves away from the people they despised as

9. *Works*, I, 321–22, 334.
10. *Satanstoe* (1845 ed.; Garden City, N.Y., n.d.), p. 472.

"fashionable," while the latter did not know how to make advances to them. Only in sophisticated societies did the intellectual "recognize the uses of the frivolous," and the frivolous know how to make their houses attractive to their betters.[11]

A similar report came from Julia Ward Howe, also a product of New York's elite society. Mrs. Howe moved to Boston in 1844 upon her marriage to Samuel Gridley Howe, the reformer and educator of the blind. As a member of New York's "four hundred," she found ready acceptance among "Boston's forty," as she put it; and in those fashionable circles she learned to be condescending toward the "transcendental people," whose language she found to be unintelligible. Thanks, however, to friendships made through her husband, she came to know quite another Boston, the world of teachers, reformers, cranks, and apostles. Her society mentors had taught her to believe that abolitionists were coarse, vulgar demagogues, but she discovered to her surprise and delight that men like Theodore Parker and even Garrison were not ogres, but thorough gentlemen.[12]

Magazine editors were among the more effective spokesmen for the gentry. George William Curtis, the "Easy Chair" editor of *Harper's Magazine*, published

11. *A Backward Glance* (New York, 1934), 68–69, 93–95.
12. *Reminiscences, 1819–1899* (Boston and New York, 1900), pp. 145–53.

a volume of essays satirizing the claims and pretensions of Fashionable Society from the gentry point of view. Why should a mere money-making talent or the accident of descent from a distinguished ancestor justify claims to an exclusive place in "society"? In a country where people were supposedly judged by their merits, the standards of fashionable society were a glaring paradox. By comparing the gentry and fashionable society with respect to standards, activities, and social outlook, Curtis was able to demonstrate that fashionable society was merely a caricature of the gentry.[13]

Nathaniel Parker Willis, editor of the New York *Home Journal,* voiced the same view that Edith Wharton was to express more than a generation later when he regretted that the Pocket Aristocracy and the Aristocracy of the Brain had not been brought together. Aspiring hostesses of the 1850's were not secure enough to risk the presence in their parlors of anyone not known to belong to the fashionable set. Yet there were in New York, Willis liked to think, enough beautiful and accomplished women, dramatists, musicians, cultivated foreigners, critics, and poets to combine with the superior men among the merchants, lawyers, and politicians to form a

13. *The Potiphar Papers* (New York, 1856).

society equal in brilliance to any that Europe could display.[14] These journalistic spokesmen resented the publicity accorded to the activities of high society. They could not appreciate the reasons why in a democratic society more attention should be paid to the affairs of the idle rich than to the constructive activities of authors, artists, and politicians.[15] Cooper agreed with Willis that gentry and social elite should coalesce and that their failure to do so was a symptom of American provincialism.

III

The lineage of the nineteenth-century gentry clearly traces back to the old eighteenth-century gentry, although there were great differences between the two classes. The eighteenth-century gentry had been truly a ruling class. It had achieved what later gentry spokesmen hoped for in vain, namely, a fusion of intellectual and social interests in a single social class. Merchants, planters, and professional men stood shoulder to shoulder, while intellectual life reflected the practical and responsible qualities that resulted from its source in men of power and prestige.

14. *Hurry-Graphs; or, Sketches of Scenery, Celebrities and Society, Taken from Life* (2nd ed.; New York, 1851), pp. 263–67.
15. *Ibid.*, pp. 316–19.

93

The disintegration of the old gentry class was a process that commenced with its division into Patriot and Tory factions in the Revolutionary era and was completed with the democratization of American society and politics in the early decades of the nineteenth century. Fragmentary accounts of this process are available to us, chiefly in the form of political histories of various states. I am persuaded, however, that party divisions in the early years of the republic did not conform neatly to social class divisions, and that the rhetoric of party warfare is not a reliable guide to the realities of social life. Although Federalism continued to represent in a more direct way the interests and attitudes of the old gentry, the Anti-Federalist party was also—at least until the War of 1812—dominated by members of the same class.[16] Dixon Ryan Fox found that the second war with England marked the demise of political Federalism in New York, and the same event may also be taken to signify roughly the disintegration of the old gentry class.

Out of the wreckage of the old gentry emerged the two nineteenth-century classes I have already described. The social-economic elite of wealthy com-

16. Cf. the remark of Gouverneur Morris: "There never was, and never will be a civilized Society without an Aristocracy." D. R. Fox, *The Decline of Aristocracy in the Politics of New York* (New York, 1919), pp. 8–22.

mercial, financial, and industrial interests allied themselves with a few descendants of distinguished older families to form the fashionable society of the seaboard cities. Because of the relative ease and speed with which new wealth was acquired, fashionable society was constantly on the defensive against the ambitious but socially untutored new rich. The pressure for admission of these elements was irresistible, and throughout the nineteenth century, the social-economic elite was obliged to digest a regularly increasing flow of raw recruits—a challenge to digestion that may well account for the sour and dyspeptic outlook on life that all too frequently characterized that class. Thanks to the democratization of politics, the social-economic elite did not inherit political leadership from the old gentry; it eschewed direct participation in politics and was content to limit its political involvement to those issues of immediate concern to its economic interests.

The cultural and intellectual responsibilities of the old gentry descended to the new nineteenth-century gentry. The status of the latter as a social class was undoubtedly jeopardized by its separation from the social-economic elite. Nevertheless, in terms of the functional and quasi-subjective criteria that we commonly employ in our ascriptions of social class, I believe that the new gentry may usefully be regarded

95

as a class. It is certain that its members were conscious of a perennial issue for all social classes, namely, the important role of the family as the custodian and transmitter of the qualities deemed to be distinctive of the class in question. Save for the chattel slaves, American classes have never been birthright classes in the full sense; but consciousness of the importance of family heritage is one good test of class consciousness, and in this respect the nineteenth-century gentry, although less conscious of family than were the social-economic elite, developed their own distinctive sense of heritage.

For clarity of presentation I have described the social-economic elite and the gentry as two distinct classes, but in fact there was partial but significant overlapping, chiefly in the larger seaboard cities. The overlap consisted of individuals and families who enjoyed status in both groups. The overlapping sectors of elite and gentry came closest to perpetuating the prestige and functions of the old eighteenth-century gentry. Holmes's famous phrase, "the Brahmin caste," would appear to refer most appositely to the overlapping sectors of Boston society. Doctor Holmes himself belonged in this group. His father, the Rev. Abiel Holmes, had married the daughter of a prominent merchant, Oliver Wendell; and Holmes in turn married Amelia Lee Jackson, daughter of Judge Charles Jackson. Connections of this quality no doubt gave Holmes a stronger sense of the value of family ties than he might otherwise have had. Yet when he came to enumerate the supposed advantages of distinguished family connections, references to wealth or fashionable social status were conspicuously absent. He spoke rather of books, art objects, and polished manners.[17] Although he unquestionably savored the advantages that his elite connections brought him, his defense of status rested upon values associated with the gentry rather than the social elite.

Intermarriage seems to have been a common method of securing status in the overlapping sectors of elite and gentry. Louis Agassiz made an elite marriage to a Cary, following the death of his first wife; his children married, respectively, a Shaw, a Higginson, and a Russell.[18] The balance of payments, so to speak, might flow either way. The marriage of elite capitalist John Murray Forbes to Emerson's daughter brought a distinction to the Forbes family that is even yet kept green.[19] These alliances produced a favored group that moved with equal assurance in either elite or gentry circles. Social discriminations of this kind might on occasion be precisely made. Frederick J.

17. *The Autocrat of the Breakfast-Table* (Boston and New York, 1892), pp. 20–22.
18. Cleveland Amory, *The Proper Bostonians* (New York, 1947), p. 184.
19. Frederick J. Stimson, *My United States* (New York, 1931), p. 111.

Stimson, for instance, tells us categorically that Holmes and Lowell had entree to elite circles but that Howells and Aldrich did not.

Whether the existence of the overlapping group, with its grasp upon the qualities and skills prized by both classes, had the hoped-for effect of civilizing the social-economic elite is a difficult question to answer. N. P. Willis thought it did, observing wistfully from New York that in Boston they would tolerate neither the rich fool nor the mere literary man.[20] Bostonians themselves were not so sure. Judge Robert Grant recalled that when Mrs. J. Montgomery Sears introduced musicales into the Boston social program, one could meet in her parlors not only one's friends but also musicians, painters, and any first-rate actors who happened to be in town. "This semi-Bohemian atmosphere," Grant observed dryly, "was highly beneficial to Boston, serving to enlarge its social outlook." But when young Grant took his cultural responsibilities so seriously as to join the Papyrus Club and spend convivial evenings in company with such Bohemians as John Boyle O'Reilly, Frank Harris, and George Makepeace Towle, his father saw fit to issue a timely warning against burning his candle at both ends.[21]

20. *Op. cit.*, pp. 12–13.
21. *Fourscore* (Boston and New York, 1934), pp. 125, 130.

In New York City, earlier in the century at least, if not in Edith Wharton's time, there was a similar if not so extensive overlapping. The elder John Jacob Astor enjoyed the society of literary men and endowed the library that bears his name. The father of Julia Ward Howe was a banker whose cultural interests drew writers, academicians, and theologians to his home. Poe was known here if not in other circles. Thomas Crawford, the sculptor, executed mantelpieces in the Ward home and married one of Ward's daughters.[22] Descendants of old gentry families of Philadelphia formed the nucleus of the overlapping group in that city. Many of them were found by the middle of the nineteenth century to be professional men of moderate incomes, while the new industrial and social leaders were uneducated men without active cultural interests.[23]

The relationship between gentility and creativity had always been a close one, although the artist, writer, or thinker was not identical with the gentleman. Their respective historical origins had been distinctly different, the gentleman originating in privilege and the creative person in humble craftsmanship. The gentleman's interest in creativity had

22. Howe, *Reminiscences*, pp. 23, 26–27, 39, 43–46, 75.
23. E. Digby Baltzell, *Philadelphia Gentlemen: The Making of a National Upper Class* (Glencoe, Ill., 1958), pp. 107–9.

99

traditionally been that of the connoisseur and sponsor. Where he cultivated the arts himself, usually as a writer or musician, he did so for his private pleasure rather than for public recognition or reward; he diverted himself in the amateur spirit. It was not until the nineteenth century that the social evolution of the gentry brought the class to the point where its association with creativity, if not wholly identical, was at least a very close one. With the separation of gentry from social-economic elite at the beginning of the century, the cultural responsibilities of the class became more direct and exclusive than before. Creative people were in turn encouraged to subscribe to the attitudes and attributes of gentility, which they did to a surprising extent. A professional tone began to replace the old amateurism. The gentry acquired a sense of cultural responsibility that led to substantial amalgamation with individuals of intellectual and creative bent. Otherwise Emerson's idealization of the gentleman would have seemed quite beside the point.

IV

Although I have connected the origins of the gentry to the breaking up of the old eighteenth-century gentry class, this was not the way the new gentry themselves preferred to view the matter. They liked to think of themselves as the spontaneous products of a free and democratic society. The founder and first editor of the *North American Review*, William Tudor, observed in 1820 that the true principles of gentility were everywhere gaining ground because of the increasing acceptance of the doctrine of original equality. Artificial distinctions of rank according to birth were coming to be regarded as barbarous, while talent, service, and merit were rapidly becoming the only acceptable basis for precedence.[24]

Cooper pointed out that in a democratic society the individual who was fortunate enough to associate with men of breeding, wealth, and education enjoyed an advantage that the mere nobleman in an aristocratic society could never know. The American gentleman possessed of wealth, manners, and education had the best his society could offer, and there was no one superior to him. "So long as society shall be governed by its ordinary and natural feelings," Cooper concluded, "it is not possible to deprive money, intelligence, and manners of their influence."[25] This conception of an "ordinary and natural" society, one without the artificially imposed distinctions of rank found in Europe, suggests an analogy with the natural economic society posited by the laissez-faire econo-

24. *Letters on the Eastern States* (New York, 1820), p. 170.
25. *Notions*, II, 389–90.

101

mists. When given free play, social laws analagous to economic laws ordained the inevitable pre-eminence of the gentry, the class of money, brains, and style. It is worth noting also that Cooper took it for granted that wealth, intelligence, and manners would always go together. The old gentry had been strikingly successful in achieving such a fusion, and Cooper revealed his old-gentry heritage as well as his status in the overlapping group in New York when he assumed that wealth and cultural interests would continue to be united. In fact, with the division between new gentry and social-economic elite they were to be separated, and the gentry correspondingly weakened in prestige and influence.

Emerson reaffirmed the prevailing view when he observed that there was a natural rank order in society in which each individual occupied the place determined by the "symmetry of his structure." Good breeding and personal superiority would always assert their claims and be recognized everywhere. A gentry was thus inevitable. The liberal social philosophy that the nineteenth-century gentry espoused was simply the practical application of the sociological conviction that a free society would provide automatically for the confirmation of the highest social and cultural values.

A free and democratic society not only found an exalted place for the gentleman in the natural order; it also furnished the social conditions for his original fabrication. It produced a "natural" gentleman as distinct from a "cultivated" or "fine" gentleman. The best thing that could be said for any society was that it provided an environment in which dignity, courage, honor, and respect for quality were nurtured. These were the basic moral attributes of the gentleman, and if a cultural region could equip its denizens with these qualities, it was accomplishing far more of real worth than the fashionable circle that adorned its members with the polite graces of the drawing room. America was accounted fortunate in possessing several cultural regions in which natural gentlemen were nurtured.

In his simplest guise the natural gentleman need not be a product of Western culture at all. He might be the savage Indian chief depicted by Cooper in *The Redskins*, "a gentleman in the best meaning of the word," whose natural gentility had developed under "the impetus of an unrestrained though savage liberty." [26] On a more sophisticated yet still relatively primitive level would be Cooper's most famous char-

26. *Works* (Leatherstocking Edition), XXVIII, 443, as quoted in Thomas F. Gossett, *Race: The History of an Idea in America* (Dallas, 1963), p. 240.

acter, Leatherstocking, the natural gentleman who was the combined product of the free forest and the first and most generous phase of the cycle of western settlement.

But these are peripheral examples that help to define the type. To the American gentry the central type and source of natural gentility was to be found among the yeomen, whether farmers or craftsmen. Early in the century, Edward Everett affirmed that the American yeomanry was "perhaps the most substantial, uncorrupted, and intelligent population on earth." [27] Nearly a century later, Barrett Wendell repeated with approval the seventeenth-century maxim of Fuller, that "a good yeoman is a gentleman in the ore." [28] The cultivated gentlemen of the gentry class, who added the refinements of a sophisticated culture to the basic moral virtues and personal attributes of the natural gentleman, were thus prepared ideologically to recognize the natural gentleman whenever they might encounter him in the flesh. The younger Josiah Quincy, a superb specimen of the Boston gentry, told how he first met Andrew Jackson. When the President toured New England in 1833 it was

27. *Orations and Speeches on Various Occasions* (4 vols.; 7th ed.; Boston, 1865), I, 17.
28. M. A. DeWolfe Howe, *Barrett Wendell and His Letters* (Boston, 1924), p. 256.

104

Quincy's duty as aide to the governor of Massachusetts to meet Jackson at the boundary of Rhode Island
and accompany him while in the state. Knowing him
only by repute as a formidable barbarian, Quincy
took the assignment with considerable foreboding.
But when they met, he saw at once that Jackson "was,
in essence, a knightly personage,—prejudiced, narrow, mistaken upon many points, it might be, but
vigorously a gentleman in his high sense of honor
and in the natural straightforward courtesies which
are easily to be distinguished from the veneer of
policy. . . ." The qualities of the President that
most impressed Quincy were his sincerity, decision,
honesty, and earnestness.[29] Jackson was only one of
the more impressive of the breed of natural gentlemen
who were the products of America's distinctive regional cultures.

In the famous Phi Beta Kappa oration of 1824
that launched his political career, Edward Everett
expatiated eloquently on the promise of a rich intellectual life inherent in American circumstances. A
free society, he affirmed, could not help but quicken
and refresh intellectual activity. In the absence of
court patronage there would be no cultural metropolis

29. *Figures of the Past from the Leaves of Old Journals* (Boston,
1926), p. 296.

105

and no deadening contrast between urbane cultivation and the rude hinterland. Each of the cultural regions of the country would spontaneously nourish the seeds of an automous intellectual activity. "These little local republics are schools of character and nurseries of mind." The intellectual potential that was scattered at random throughout the entire population would be nourished by universal education and stimulated by the challenge of free institutions.[30]

V

Unlike the social elite, who attached great importance to distinguished family connections and courted much ridicule by their industrious search for illustrious ancestors, the gentry were content to seek their origins in the autonomous cultural regions of America. In the East, such regions existed from early colonial times, while in the Middle West they might extend back little more than a generation. Memoirs and reminiscences provide a principal source for the gentry's sense of their regional cultural heritage. Autobiography as a conventional literary genre is hardly more than a century old. Beginning about 1840, there was a very great increase in the writing of such

30. *Orations*, I, 9–44.

reminiscences, reaching flood proportions in the twentieth century.[31] These autobiographies, many of which were written by persons of gentry-class status, are a richly detailed record of the origins of the class; and they reveal a surprisingly uniform kind of early experience.

The gentry class survived for only about a century, the span of two lifetimes. If we take the second generation to consist of those who came to adulthood after the Civil War, it was this generation that left the fuller record of appreciation of its heritage. A couple of illustrations will suffice. Senator George Frisbie Hoar of Massachusetts, referring piously to his birthplace, expressed the conviction that the world had never seen a better example of pure and beautiful democracy than that provided by the town of Concord from 1826 to the Civil War. There was neither wealth nor poverty; neither mansions nor hovels. Richer and poorer mingled on terms of personal intimacy. If any citizen took precedence, it was by virtue of personal worth. The population, "of good English stock," was as permanent as in any spot in Europe. Gentle blood flowed in the veins of many. "It is interesting to observe," reflected the senator, "how little the char-

31. Louis Kaplan, *A Bibliography of American Autobiographies* (Madison, Wisconsin, 1961). My generalization is based on a sample study of 10 per cent of the titles listed in Kaplan.

acter of the gentleman or gentlewoman in our New England people is affected by the pursuit, for generations, of humble occupations, which in other countries are deemed degrading." For generations these men and women of Concord would perform manual labor without producing the effect on character that would follow in England or Germany. Whenever a college education became available to a favored individual, he would respond successfully to the challenge and rise from the anonymity of his forebears.[32]

A similar report came from Lucy Larcom, the poetess of the textile mills, who grew up on Cape Ann, and whose ancestors since the seventeenth century had been humble farmers and sailors. They "accepted with sturdy dignity an inheritance of hard work and the privileges of poverty, leaving the same bequest to their descendants." She believed that "to have been born of people of integrity and profound faith in God, is better than to have inherited material wealth of any kind." These humble yeomen had carefully preserved the religious and literary heritage of Anglo-American civilization. Poor though they were, the Larcom family had provided themselves with books and newspapers. Lucy's precocious literary bent was nourished by Watt's hymns, Shakespeare, Coleridge,

32. *Autobiography of Seventy Years* (New York, 1903), pp. 40–41.

Wordsworth, and Bryant. "The happiness of our lives," she recalled, "was rooted in the stern, vigorous virtues of the people we lived among, drawing thence its bloom and song and fragrance. There was granite in their character and belief, but it was granite that could smile in the sunshine and clothe itself with flowers." [33]

Veneration for the regional heritage was doubtless due in part to sentimentalized recollections of the simple way of life that still prevailed in the early nineteenth century, especially in humble farm homes. Hardship and discomfort tended to be forgotten, while memories of the open fire and co-operative family enterprises invested the past with a nostalgic glow. When the iron stove was introduced and the great fireplaces were shut up, an era had ended. As Lucy Larcom put it, shaggy Romance abdicated and elegant Commonplace was enthroned. [34]

With minor variations of theme, these appreciations of the regional heritage come from many parts of the country. Cooper's account of the Hudson Valley region, where the ethnic stocks were Dutch and English, included a careful analysis of the respective social-psychological qualities of these two races. Even

33. *A New England Girlhood* (Boston and New York, 1889), pp. 19, 91–92, 118–20, 126–36.
34. *Ibid.*, pp. 22–23.

relatively new country like Indiana quickly developed a regional culture that would be recalled in later years through a haze of fond memories. Robert Underwood Johnson, whose boyhood was spent in Wayne County, recalled the genuine literary interests of the local bench and bar, where everyone wrote verses, and the recesses of court sessions would be filled with talk of Byron and Scott. In reminiscing about the simple pleasures of those times, Johnson expressed the conviction that all of the gentry must have shared: "Surely there is no soil for the growth of character like the happiness of childhood." [35]

One of the reasons why these cultural regions so uniformly fostered a happy childhood is found in the prevailing form and spirit of family life in the early nineteenth century. It is no mere truism to say that the cultural region was a region composed of families. In virtually every autobiography one finds the family the dominant social institution. This was true for city-bred as well as rural children. It was of course the inevitable consequence of a conventional way of looking at life from the perspective of a personal career. From this perspective the school, the church, and other childhood associations outside of the family, to say nothing of the more remote social

35. Cooper, *Satanstoe, passim; Remembered Yesterdays* (Boston, 1923), pp. 25–48.

institutions, did not compare with the family as a dominating influence upon childhood. Nevertheless, there were special reasons why the family environment of the early republic should have bulked so large in retrospective consciousness, and why the autobiographical form of literature should have been so appropriate for expressing the sense of the peculiar importance of family nurture.

Family structure was in the process of transformation from the patriarchical, extended family of colonial times, with the source of authority firmly located in the male head, to the modern nuclear family of parents and dependent children in which authority, if any, largely reflects the accidents of personality. In this transformation the point reached at the beginning of the nineteenth century might well deserve to be designated the golden age of the American family. The arbitrary and legal authority of the male head of the family was being relaxed, while the moral traditions of the community still invested his role with dignity and power. Out of this relaxation emerged many trends of social and economic consequence of which the emancipated lady and romanticized childhood were among the more important.

In all societies social class distinctions are actually articulated in differing patterns of family behavior, and in most societies classes are firmly rooted in

111

hereditary distinctions among families. Even in the fluid conditions of modern American society, so Lloyd Warner tells us, class differences are actually differences among families. Whatever the social status of the head of the family, the other members occupy the same status; and if his status changes, they change with him. The old eighteenth-century gentry were as successful as any American class has ever been in rooting the class in a durable web of family relationships, sustained through several generations. In Virginia and New York, and to a lesser degree in the seaboard towns of New England, clusters of old gentry families were relatively successful in molding the behavior of their members (including marriage) so as to assure class continuity. But the control was by no means complete, for a steady stream of outsiders was constantly entering the class by virtue of commercial or professional success, confirmed by intermarriage of children.

After the separation of the new gentry from the social-economic elite, it was the latter that continued to value and reward descent from distinguished forbears, while the gentry tended to identify family with region. The heritage of moral and religious ideals of the region was perpetuated in families, and whatever merit the family possessed was largely determined by its success in perpetuating these values. It mattered relatively little who one's ancestors were so long as

112

it was apparent that they had faithfully transmitted the heritage.[36] Although the new gentry was more a functional than a birthright class, its members liked to think of themselves as the products of a cultural heritage perpetuated by the families of the region.

The pride of family commonly displayed by the gentry was thus in effect the due recognition of accomplishment. John Adams once remarked that he had never heard of a great man who had not had a good mother, and that wherever distinction persisted in families through successive generations, the choice of wives was the decisive factor. Thus successful playing of the role of mother, with all of its psychological, moral, and social implications, rather than blood descent was presumed to determine the success of the family in perpetuating the values of the community. The family became the most important educational institution in the sense that the supreme lessons of morality and character as well as healthy habits of work and social relations were learned under its auspices.[37]

36. Lucy Larcom: "I am proud of my unlettered forefathers, who were also too humbly proud to care whether their names would be remembered or not; for they were God-fearing men, and had been persecuted for their faith. . . ."—*op. cit.*, p. 19.

37. The most eloquent and extensive claim known to me for the success of the early-nineteenth-century family was made by John Dewey in his famous lectures, *The School and Society* (Phoenix ed.; Chicago, n.d. [originally published, 1899]), pp. 7–12.

Whatever may have been the corrosive effects upon the family of economic opportunity, spatial and social mobility, and the spirit of democracy,[38] these same forces had an even more decisive effect upon such other basic institutions as state, church, and local community. The family withstood these pressures relatively well. No doubt certain of its traditional features as an extended kinship system were weakened, but this very fact served to uncover and dramatize the nuclear core. Many of the functions of what Robin Williams calls the "trustee family" were still retained by the early-nineteenth-century rural family, notably its share in economic production, education, government, religion, and social security.[39] Whatever it may have lost in the way of authority, the emerging nuclear family more than made up in sentiment. In popular songs and fiction the home life of the early nineteenth century was celebrated as never before or since. And by the same token, Harriet Beecher Stowe and other writers were able to invest the broken home with sentiments of anguish generated by the freeing of the emotion of love at the heart of the nuclear

38. Arthur W. Calhoun, *A Social History of the American Family* (3 vols. in 1; New York, 1945), II, 51–77, 136–37.
39. *American Society: A Sociological Interpretation* (New York, 1956), pp. 76–77; but not the control of marriage by elders.

family from the cloak of authority that the traditional family had previously wrapped about it.[40]

Out of these changing circumstances of family life emerged the autonomous world of childhood, a world to be recalled in later life with such nostalgic pleasure. One of those who probed his memories most sensitively was William Dean Howells, whose boyhood in the 1840's had been spent in the small town of Hamilton on the banks of the Miami in Ohio.[41] Although the people were primarily of Southern origin, their social relations displayed the same simple equalitarianism found in rural New England. The subtle differences of status of which a growing boy began to become aware do not seem to have intruded significantly on his consciousness. The real world in which he lived was the world of boys where such distinctions were not recognized. It was a spacious and richly furnished world that had little to do with the adult world, although we glimpse beneath it the secure, sustaining arms of the family. We have long recognized the age as one in which significant steps toward the emancipation of women were taken, and

40. *Uncle Tom's Cabin* and *Old Town Folks* thoroughly exploit the theme of the broken home. Cf. Ralph H. Gabriel, *The Course of American Democratic Thought* (2nd ed.; New York, 1956), pp. 6–7.
41. *A Boy's Town* (New York and London, 1890).

it is time to acknowledge that a similar emancipation of children was occurring.

Howells assumed that the world of boys was everywhere and always the same, with its universal unwritten laws and usages.[42] It seems more likely, however, that his generation enjoyed a more commodious and happier childhood than had been known before. Social evolution had reached the point where the portion of the life cycle assigned to boyhood was clearly marked off and granted its own independence. The earlier tendency to treat children as young adults was slowly giving way to the recognition that childhood had its own characteristics and rights. Out of this recognition was to come the twofold revolution in pedagogy and child psychology that distinguished the later decades of the nineteenth century.[43] The rapid extension of common schooling must have helped to define childhood by assigning to it a distinctive educational activity, however cursory.

42. *Ibid.*, p. 67.
43. Ruth Elson, in her book *Guardians of Tradition: American Schoolbooks of the Nineteenth Century* (Lincoln, Neb., 1964), pp. 2–6, has shown that the school texts commonly in use prior to about 1830 made no concession to childhood in terms of vocabulary or sophistication. Monica Kiefer concluded from her study of children's books (*American Children through Their Books, 1700–1835* [Philadelphia, 1948], p. 1) that the child emerged from the adult's world and achieved recognition as a distinct type of personality with rights of his own at about 1835.

116

But whatever the causes may have been, Howells clearly established the autonomous domain of boyhood and proceeded to probe its character. He found its essence to be a condition of savagery as contrasted with the civilized state of adulthood. The savagery consisted in the boy's inability to "do" the things he conceived in his imagination. Unlike the civilized adult, he did not relate efficiently to his natural environment; he did not clearly grasp what practical things he could not do. A boy could only imitate, and it was always easier to imitate evil than good; hence he was all too frequently foolish, thoughtless, and mischievous. Life was a serious business for these boys. "They lived in a state of outlawry, in the midst of invisible terrors, and they knew no rule but that of might." [44] In such a savage world a code of honor grew up, not unlike the code of the natural gentleman by which Susquesus and Leatherstocking had lived and died. The niceties of manners may have been neglected, and boys may have been wanting in generosity, but in other essentials their code revealed the indigenous source of gentility. Lying and cheating were despised; and boys were always respectful of women. Such a boyhood, recollected in tranquility, seemed an idyllic and romantic primitivism. To How-

44. *Op. cit.,* p. 211.

ells, the intensity of the pleasures of a summer's day in boyhood would never again be equaled.[45] The boy had had the best of two worlds: the family where affection and security were provided; and the boy's world, a carefully delimited neighborhood teeming with the challenge and excitement of conflict and the unknown. Howells shows us what the sociological raw materials were, and it remained only for his friend Mark Twain to convert them into his great fictional portrayals of boyhood.

The residual effect of such recollections upon the gentry of Howells' generation must have strengthened, if it was not the principal cause of, the nostalgia for a better and happier time that permeated the thought of the gentry at the end of the nineteenth century. The recollected happiness of youth that emerges in so many of the autobiographies of the period easily spilled over into the more general impression that former times had been better with respect to the nurturing of the gentry values of freedom, independence, and good fellowship.

The historic function of the gentry was to articulate the democratic ideal; to confound the skeptics and

45. Modern novelists and readers who take it for granted that life begins at puberty must find this quaint conviction of Howells' only another indication of his Victorian prudery.

118

prove to the world that democracy and high culture were mutually compatible. But so long as they constituted a social class, the gentry were unable to merge themselves completely in the democratic mass of the community. They expected to furnish leadership by virtue of their gentility; and they were increasingly conscious of the fact that the community rejected their leadership. This fundamental ambiguity was present in the gentry mind from the beginning, running as a leitmotif through all their discussions. As the century advanced, they were thrust back upon their own resources, and the note of disillusionment and pessimism sounded ever more clearly. When eventually the realization spread among surviving members of the class that the old cultural regions were no longer nurturing the qualities of natural gentility, that the original ethnic stocks were being replaced by alien races, their despair was complete. Barrett Wendell's anguished cry in 1904 represented the death throes of his class. "The racial agony in which we are being strangled by invading aliens, who shall inherit the spirit of us, grows heavier with me, as the end of me—and of ours—comes nearer." [46]

46. Howe, *Wendell*, p. 162.

119

RUSSEL B. NYE

History and Literature:
Branches of the Same Tree

RUSSEL B. NYE

History and Literature:
Branches of the Same Tree

The title of this paper possibly sounds old-fashioned at a time when history departments are often found in colleges of social science and when historians draw sustenance from the Social Science Research Council. Certainly it would not have sounded so a few generations ago, when it was assumed that history and literature were not only branches of the same tree, but that they both stemmed closely together from the main trunk of human knowledge. To the historians and literary artists of a century ago, their function was in essence much the same—to interpret experience, for the purpose of guiding and elevating man. As a reviewer in the *Boston Quarterly Review* wrote in 1838, historians were

seers upon the watch towers, gazing with serene eye upon the moral firmament, reading the aspect of the lights and shadows which alternate in the moral heavens, solving the problems, interpreting the prophecies, and opening the parables which are written in the history of man, which are uttered by the experience of society.

This is a large order, of course, but it is indicative of the range that the nineteenth-century historian expected to cover; his aim, like the literary artist's, was the ordering and interpreting of experience to some useful and civilized end. The field of scholarship was shared, in those days, by novelists and historians and poets and philosophers, who bowed like gentlemen—as Bancroft might to Cooper and Emerson, or Macaulay to Scott and Carlyle— as they met each other crossing it. The area they explored, now trampled with the footprints of other disciplines, from sociology, economics, psychology, anthropology (and sometimes, even, statistics), was common soil that all sowed and harvested. Because the nineteenth century believed man's mind to be controlled by reason and imagination working in harmonious relation, it believed poets, historians, and philosophers could establish relations among themselves with ease and exactness. Macaulay, writing in the *Edinburgh Review* at the beginning of his career, explained that history

lies on the confines of two distinct territories. It is under the jurisdiction of two hostile powers, and like other districts similarly situated, it is ill defined, ill cultivated, and ill regulated. Instead of being equally shared between its two rulers, the Reason and the Imagination, it falls alternately under the sole and absolute dominion of each. It is sometimes fiction; it is sometimes theory.

One can better understand Macaulay's point when it is remembered that as he wrote, Sir Walter Scott had just published his twenty-ninth novel—though it is certain that Macaulay considered Scott fiction rather than theory, and imaginative rather than rational.

Emerson, in his essay "History" (1841), defined literature as "fable," created by the imagination, and history as "experience," interpreted by the reason. Both were records of the "one mind, common to all individual men." George Bancroft, writing in 1854, saw both poet and historian as grand interpreters of what God meant by His world. Bancroft granted priority to the poet, who "catches the first beam of light" that flows from the Divine Mind rather than finding it, as the historian does, in the past; but the chronological order of revelation he did not find important. "It is because God is visible in history that its office is the noblest except that of the poet," he wrote.

History, as she reclines in the lap of eternity, sees the mind of humanity itself engaged in formative efforts. . . . Of all the pursuits that require analysis, therefore, history stands first. It is equal to philosophy; for as certainly as the actual bodies forth the ideal, so certainly does history contain philosophy. It is grander than the natural sciences; for its study is man, the last work of creation, and the most perfect in its relation with the Infinite.[1]

History and literature, their nineteenth-century practitioners agreed, offered a continuous, integrated,

1. "The Progress of Mankind," *Literary and Historical Miscellanies* (New York, 1855), pp. 492–93.

125

selective narrative of experience that had meaning and relevance to man's condition; both attempted to distil out of experience some understanding of the relation between act and reaction, cause and effect. Both were concerned, Bancroft told the American Historical Association in 1886, with "the discerning of the presence of law in the actions of rational beings." Both were assured of the importance of their relationship, confident of their common purpose and optimistic of their chances of achieving it.

The divorcement of history and literature came, of course, with the rise of "scientific history" during the latter decades of the nineteenth century, a story too familiar to need recounting in detail here.[2] A distinction arose between "literary" and "scientific" historians, between the followers of Hegel and the followers of Ranke—that is, between those who believed that the writing of history began with a theory that might make order out of the course of events; and those who believed it began with a gathering of information about events from which certain justifiable generalizations about them might emerge.

The American historical tradition of the first three-quarters of the century, represented by such men as

2. A useful summary is W. Stull Holt, "The Idea of Scientific History in America," *Journal of the History of Ideas,* I (June, 1940), 252–62.

Bancroft, Motley, Prescott, and Parkman, belonged in the first school; they searched for what Bancroft called "a pervading principle" that gave "continuity √ and utility" to history. The younger men who followed them assumed that the principle grew out of the facts; Ranke, they were fond of saying, customarily began his lectures with the words, "Gentlemen, I will simply tell you how it was." (It is interesting to note that Ranke, according to some stories, first began to evolve his criteria of scientific historicity after his shock at reading Scott's *Quentin Durward* and finding it historically inaccurate.) The men who learned their historical theory in the Teutonic school assumed—as their predecessors would not have— that it was actually possible to tell "how it was," exactly, precisely, objectively, fully. The older nineteenth-century historian could not do this, for he could only imagine, and by imagining do no more than guess.

The distinction between "scientific" and "literary" history, as the case was argued during the period, was not a completely clear one; the words involved had a number of meanings. To some the word "scientific" meant merely objectivity, a lack of prejudgment in the use of evidence. To others it suggested analogies between history and the physical and biological sciences, a search for laws that explained historical

127

development as the laws of natural selection or entropy explained sequences of events in science. However they defined "science" in history, these historians agreed that the "literary" histories written by the early nineteenth century were unacceptable by the new standards. They did not mean that history might not be written with skill and attention to the use of language. They meant that narrative history whose interpretations depended on the personal point of view of the historian, and whose meanings were influenced by his philosophical-theological beliefs, was really not history at all, but literature, which was a quite different thing. They did not believe that the historian should attempt to be a conscious artist in the telling of his tale. He should be an observer, a generalizer, beguiled not by the dramatic style of Parkman or the sermonized rhetoric of Bancroft, but a narrator of what actually happened, and only that. The historian was to be honest and thorough and impartial; he should not write too well (a warning not always necessary), though he should write as clearly, say, as the writer of a laboratory report or a sociological abstract.

These "scientific" historians were not against literature; they simply did not believe that the processes by which it was created or the form it took had any significant relation to the business of history. Some historians, in fact, became highly incensed about this, scornfully rejecting "the filio-pietists and hero-worshippers" whose histories were only "haphazard guesses of no scientific validity." Charles McLean Andrews once called George Bancroft's work, the most popular history of his time, the product of "ignorance and national bias . . . , nothing less than a crime against historical truth"—and overly-harsh indictment, certainly, but one that illustrates the depth of feeling the argument over history once aroused.[3]

The emergence of historical scientism also helped to encourage the rise of the professional historian, who conceived of himself not as co-worker of the poet or philosopher, but rather as cousin of the scientist. He hoped to avoid the unscientific—even the artistic—and to emphasize those qualities of his craft that were least like those of the literary man. The true historian, wrote Charles M. Andrews, pursued "his experiments just as does the investigator in the laboratory." The study of history, agreed Charles Francis Adams, "closely allied to astronomy, geology, and physics . . . , seeks a scientific basis from which the rise and fall of races and dynasties will be seen merely as phases of a consecutive process of evolution." His model was the scientist, his method, inductive. If the

3. A. S. Eisenstadt, *Charles McLean Andrews* (New York, 1956) cites numerous similar examples.

historian was to be a true social scientist, there was no place in his work for those inward intuitions that motivated the artist, or for those things he held in common with the literary practitioner.

The difference between the new "scientific" historical procedure and the older "literary" tradition was perhaps nowhere better illustrated at the time than by Henry Adams and Theodore Roosevelt. Products of much the same age and class, though Adams was the older man, they looked at the craft of history from widely different angles. Roosevelt, the talented amateur, considered history to be—as had Parkman, his much-admired mentor—an essentially literary task. Adams, strongly influenced by Ranke, approached it from the opposite direction. His illustrious predecessors he dismissed as mere storytellers; of Bancroft's constitutional history he once remarked, with refined arrogance, that he at least found the appendixes and footnotes interesting. "Since Gibbon," Adams wrote in his *Education*,

> the spectacle was almost a scandal. History had lost the sense of shame. It was a hundred years behind the experimental sciences. For all serious purposes, it was less instructive than Walter Scott and Alexander Dumas.

Adams, who wanted to transfer scientific certainty to history, called for a "law of phase" as valid for historical study as Willard Gibbs's famous law for the study of physics. He wanted apparatus that, he wrote, might "hasten the coming of an epoch when man should study his own history in the same spirit and by the same methods with which he studied the formation of a crystal."

Yet whatever his disclaimers, the history Adams did write was certainly not devoid of literary quality; his *History of the United States During the Administrations of Jefferson and Madison* (written, true, before his theory of history had fully hardened) displayed much of the imaginativeness and stylistic care that he scoffed at in Bancroft. He was a sophisticated stylist, with a sense of balance and form combined with a kind of sardonic urbanity that was distinctively Adams. His swift and skilful characterization of the New England Federalists, for example, is hard to surpass:

The obstinacy of the race was never better shown than when with the sunlight of the nineteenth century bursting upon them, these resolute sons of granite and ice turned their faces from the sight, and smiled in their sardonic way at the folly or wickedness of men who could pretend to believe the world improved because henceforth the ignorant and vicious were to rule the United States and govern the churches and schools of New England.[4]

4. *History of the United States during the Administration of Jefferson and Madison* (New York, 1890), I, 87.

131

Adams, however, considered himself a professional, not an amateur—and not an academic, if we are to trust his thrusts at his native Harvard—of a kind that Theodore Roosevelt was not. Roosevelt, far from rejecting the literary-historical tradition of Motley and Prescott, revered it; he could see no reason why the new so-called scientific history and the older belletristic variety could not exist together and reinforce each other's virtues. Good history, he once observed, is simply a presentation of scientific matter in literary form.

> The great historian of the future will have easy access to innumerable facts patiently gathered by tens of thousands of investigators, whereas the great historian of the past had very few facts, and often had to gather most of these himself. . . . Yet even with these instruments he can not do as good work as the best of the elder historians unless he has vision and imagination, the power to grasp what is essential and to reject the infinitely more numerous nonessentials, the power to embody ghosts, to put flesh and blood on dry bones, to make dead men living before our eyes. In short, he must have the power to take the science of history and turn it into literature.[5]

The Winning of the West, begun in 1889, showed more than any other of his books the influence of what the critic Brander Matthews called approvingly "the result of deliberate literary art employed to present

5. *History as Literature and Other Essays* (New York, 1913), pp. 15–16.

the result of honest scientific inquiry." What Roosevelt could do, in this traditional literary-historical vein, showed considerable talent. Dealing with George Rogers Clark and his fording of the Wabash River before Vincennes, Roosevelt wrote in prose that his master Parkman might well have applauded:

The night was bitterly cold, for there was a heavy frost, and the ice formed half an inch thick round the edges and in the smooth water. But the sun rose bright and glorious, and Clark, in words, told his stiffened, famished, half-frozen followers that the evening would surely see them at the goal of their hopes. Without waiting for an answer, he plunged into the water, and they followed him with a cheer. . . . Before them lay a broad sheet of water, covering what was known as the Horse Shoe Plain; the floods had made it a shallow lake four miles across, unbroken by so much as a handsbreadth of dry land. On its farther side was a dense wood. Clark led breast-high in the water with fifteen or twenty of the strongest men next to him. About the middle of the plain the cold and exhaustion told so on the weaker men that the little dugouts plied frantically to and fro to save the more helpless from drowning. Those, who though weak, could still move onwards, clung to the stronger, and struggled ahead. When they at last reached the woods, the water became so deep that it was to the shoulders of the tallest; but the weak and those of low stature could now cling to the bushes and old logs, until the canoes were able to ferry them to a spot of dry land. Many on reaching the shore fell flat on their faces, and could move no farther.[6]

6. *The Works of Theodore Roosevelt* (Memorial Edition; New York, 1923–26), X, 380–87.

This is vivid, planned, artistic prose. The sentences are direct and swift; the details are concrete, the writing energetic, the masculine rhythmic pattern suited to the action. The twin themes of water and cold run through the passage as a refrain, and the alliteration of the final sentence is hardly accidental. This is essentially the "story-telling" history that historical scientism rejected.

Roosevelt was quite conscious of the rift between the old and new schools of historical thinking, and when he spoke at the American Historical Association meeting in 1912, he chose as his topic "History as Literature," hoping to explain the continuity that he believed American historical writing could not afford to lose. "Because history, science, and literature have all become specialized," he said, "the theory now is that science is definitely severed from literature and that history must follow suit. Not only do I refuse to accept this as true for history, but I do not accept it as true for science." He focused his address on his conviction that the literary artist and the historian had too much in common to justify their separation; history "must not be treated as something set off by itself . . . , as a branch of learning bound to the past by the shackles of an iron conservatism." [7] It was the aim of both literature and history, he emphasized,

7. *History as Literature and Other Essays,* pp. 8, 21.

to clothe past experience with imaginative reality, to build, as he called it, "an edifice that both charms and teaches."

I have taken some time to consider the change in attitude that marked the rise of scientific history in the years after 1880 because it marked the first real divorcement of the historical from the literary art since the Renaissance; and because the argument between scientism and literature was, in the main, both overemphasized and misunderstood. Under the label of science, the historian demanded not art but facts, facts, facts; he wanted plausibility and predictability, not "philosophy teaching by example" but neither teaching nor philosophy. History, as Ranke once said in a sentence that must have rung through a thousand seminar rooms in the nineties, was "merely to show what actually occurred." This point of view triumphed briefly, until it seemed to some, as it had to Roosevelt, that by its uncompromising anti-artistic bias, history tended to surrender more than it gained. Until it began to move, some argued, back toward the stream of the arts and away from its too-close proximity to the sciences, it stood in danger of losing a good deal of its vitality and relevance. It is interesting to note that even those new-style historians who had something to say, and who had some skill in saying it, did not elicit the popular confidence

135

possessed by those they displaced. Though Channing and von Holst were better scholars, the best-selling historian of the nineties was John Fiske, who was more public philosopher than historian, but who said what he had to say with verve and inventiveness.

Professional historians, naturally, soon recognized that possibly something had been lost. George B. Adams, in his presidential address to the American Historical Association in 1908, expressed the hope that the next generation of historians might once more take up those questions "thus far left to the poets, philosophers, and theologians." Albert Bushnell Hart titled his address to the Association in 1909 "Imagination in History," [8] warning that

The analogy of the natural sciences may be pushed too far. . . . Facts as facts, however carefully selected, scientific treatment in itself, however necessary for the ascertainment of truth, are no more history than recruits arrayed in battalions are an army.

By the time that Hart made his plea for the imagination, about all that could be said about history as a science seemed to have been said; many historians were beginning to modify some of the more positive claims of the scientific method without actually so admitting. Henry Adams' *Letter to American Teachers*

8. *American Historical Review,* XV (January, 1910), 227–57.

of History, which appeared in 1910, was the last full-scale attempt to scientize historical writing. At the same time, Carl Becker publicly suspected that those historians who claimed to deal only in "facts" were not really so sure of what they were, that they might be "only mental images of pictures which the historian makes in order to comprehend it." [9] William Sloane, who was once Bancroft's secretary, comparing history with science in 1912, found that science was not so exact and predictable as it claimed to be, and perhaps not so exemplary a model as it appeared.[10]

Since that time, neither historians nor literary artists have considered their aims incompatible nor their arts compartmentalized. Both recognize that creativeness belongs to both literature and history, that it is neither impossible nor unfashionable to write with accuracy and distinction. Allan Nevins has put it well:

Certain virtues of literary form are as vital to a complete presentation of historical truth as are certain virtues of scientific method. The historian can no more ascertain the

9. See Charlotte Smith, *Carl Becker: On History and the Climate of Opinion* (Ithaca, N. Y., 1956), pp. 71–75.

10. Herman Ausubel, *Historians and Their Craft* (New York, 1950), p. 216.

truth about the past and convey it to the reader without literary power than without scientific discipline.[11]

These common literary and artistic values appear in the best historical writing of our generation. The line between literature and history has often been crossed; Theodor Mommsen and Winston Churchill received Nobel Prizes for literature, though what they wrote was history. "The discipline of attempting to say something gracefully and effectively," writes George Kennan,

> and in such a way as to bring out the deeper and more subtle tones, seems to be helpful to the scientific essence of history, refining, rather than corrupting, the scientific conscience. . . . It is history as science *and* literature, not history as science alone, which reaches beyond the specialized reader, contributes to the public understanding of the past, and lives in historical memory.[12]

If we agree that the relationship between literature and history is a necessary and a valid one, we may proceed to examine that relationship more thoroughly, for it is not a simple or uncomplicated one. The relationship exists, I believe, at three levels. At its most obvious, this relationship arises from the form of ex-

11. "The Struggle to Make the Past Alive," *New York Times Book Review*, January 13, 1952.
12. "It's History, but Is It Literature?" *New York Times Book Review*, April 26, 1959. © 1959 by The New York Times. Reprinted by permission.

pression common to both. The historian and the literary artist use language to express what they explain and conjecture, and they use it symbolically, to express more than the words alone mean. The historian, like the poet and novelist, is aware of the metaphoric resources of language, and he draws upon them for both meaning and strength, as the scientist and the social scientist may not. If I were to choose the simplest reason why history belongs with the arts rather than with the sciences, it would be its consciousness of the wider dimensions of language.

Language, then, is the most common meeting place of the two, and that the historian is at his best when his prose is closest to art, few would argue. It is possible to write history in mediocre prose, of course, in the sense that one may find in it those "facts" that make up the skeleton of history. But on the other hand, it would seem virtually impossible to write good history in bad prose, since the qualities that demand literary skill prevent a really good historian from being a really bad stylist. Samuel Eliot Morison twenty years ago, in a classic little essay called "History as a Literary Art," warned the profession against emulating those

who have risen to positions of eminence by writing dull, solid, valuable monographs . . . , teach graduate students to write dull, solid, valuable monographs like theirs; the road

139

to academic security is that of writing dull, solid, valuable monographs.[13]

Symmetry and clarity of design, direct and concrete prose, progression and organization, and sympathy with the dynamics of language are essential equipment for success in either history or literature.

There is a second level of relationship between history and literature, one somewhat more intricate than that deriving from language. This arises from the fact that both history and literature are records of internal and external experience. Both attempt to gain from experience some kind of insight into the quality, mood, tempo, and personality of life—not just the *fact* of the past but the *feel* of it, the total recreation of time and place that history and literature strive to embody. The Persian expedition on which Xenophon went was a minor episode in a minor, ancient war; but the shout that went up from the ten thousand as they suddenly saw the wine-dark sea that led them home is one of the great moments in historical writing because it recreates for us an authentic piece of past experience. There was a Warden of the Marches named Roland who died in a skirmish with some Basque raiders centuries ago; but we still hear his horn at Roncevalles, and we know something more of the age of chivalry because of its sound, just as we

13. *By Land and by Sea* (New York, 1953), p. 291.

know something of the dark mood of Anglo-Saxon life because Beowulf wrestled a witch from the sea in the castle of a Geatish King. On hearing the news of Lincoln's death, an American poet walked out into the night from his Long Island cottage and wove the night-song of a bird, the stars, and the perfume of lilacs into an elegy that tells us more about that historical instant than we could ever otherwise know. "You shall make me feel what periods you have lived," Emerson told the writer; this vital quality of imaginative evo-cation, accomplished by history's recreation and lit-erature's renewal of the universal elements of the hu-man experience, is essential to the art of both.

To do this, documents are not enough for the his-torian. We cannot fully understand the ambiance of nineteenth-century Boston without William Dean Howells, or that of New York without Stephen Crane and Edith Wharton. Dreiser's and Farrell's and Nelson Algren's Chicago; the suburbia of F. Scott Fitzgerald and John Cheever; Sinclair Lewis' small-town Main Street and John O'Hara's smalltown Penn-sylvania; Flannery O'Connor's Georgia and William Faulkner's Mississippi—the list is a long one, easily extended. The broken cry of the slave girl Cassy, in Harriet Beecher Stowe's *Uncle Tom's Cabin*— "There's nothing here but sin, and long, long de-spair!"—tells us things about slavery and its impact on the human soul that no study of plantation records

141

can. Whittier (who was a major poet only when deeply
moved) gave in *Laus Deo!*, written on hearing the
first news of the Emancipation Proclamation, the virtually complete expression of the religious-reform
spirit that underlay much of abolitionism. In his
ten stanzas we catch, as nowhere else, the sense of the
unrelenting, evangelistic, Old Testament grimness of
the crusade that he and Garrison and others waged
against the sin of slavery:

> For the Lord
> On the Whirlwind is abroad;
> In the earthquake he has spoken;
> He has smitten with His thunder
> The iron walls asunder,
> And the gates of brass are broken!

> It is done!
> In the circuit of the sun
> Shall the sound thereof go forth.
> It shall bid the sad rejoice,
> It shall give the dumb a voice,
> It shall belt with joy the earth!

> Ring and swing,
> Bells of joy! On morning's wing
> Send the song of praise abroad!
> With a sound of broken chains
> Tell the nations that He reigns,
> Who alone is Lord and God!

What lies behind Mark Twain's description of Huck Finn's first sight of Phelps's farm in pre–Civil War Louisiana is something that Ulrich B. Phillips could never include in his admirable work. The first deep look into the dark pit of racial tensions in the nineteenth century comes in Twain's *Pudd'nhead Wilson*; the underlying implication of Huck Finn is as important a historical fact as *Plessy* v. *Ferguson*. To explore the meanings of nineteenth-century Americanism, one finds few better sources than Henry James's *The American* or *The Ambassadors*. One understands the age of Jackson the better for knowing Emerson's "Self-Reliance" and "The American Scholar." Frank Norris' truncated trilogy, *The Pit* and *The Octopus*, tell us things we need to know about the whys and wherefores of the struggle over constricted opportunities and political influences that disturbed economic life in the eighties and after. Without a story such as Hamlin Garland's "Under The Lion's Paw" we cannot fully comprehend the smouldering anger beneath the Populist revolt. Garland's description of a Midwestern farm, written in 1887, recreates what the Granger and the Farmer's Alliance felt in a way that convention speeches and newspaper stories cannot:

It was humble enough—a small white house, story-and-a-half structure, with a wing, set in the midst of a few locust trees; a small, drab-colored barn, with a sagging ridge pole;

143

a barnyard full of mud, in which a few cows were standing, fighting the flies and waiting to be milked. An old man was pumping water at the well; the pigs were squealing from a pen nearby; a child was crying. . . . He could hear a woman's fretful voice, and the impatient jerk and jar of kitchen things, indicative of ill temper and worry. . . . [He] went slowly round the corner of the house, past a vilely smelling rain barrel, toward the west. A gray-haired woman was sitting in a rocking chair on the porch, her hands in her lap, her eyes fixed on the faintly yellow sky. . . . There was sorrow, resignation, and a sort of dumb despair in her attitude.

If one wishes to know why "Sockless" Jerry Simpson or Ignatius Donnelly or William Jennings Bryan existed as they did, part of the answer lies here. Certainly, one may catch the full meanings of the confident expansiveness of America's great Golden Day in Longfellow's "Psalm of Life," which in a few stanzas sums up the mood of an era. And with it, one ought to know Melville's agonizing struggle with the problems that Longfellow so blithely solved, and Hawthorne's preoccupation with that darker side of human nature that Emerson never saw. That this works both ways goes without saying. Just as Stephen Crane's *Red Badge of Courage* adds dimension to our understanding of the Civil War, so we ought to recognize that without somebody like Bruce Catton we cannot know all we should about Crane. To feel fully what Garland meant, we ought to put his work into the frame of reference that John D. Hicks provides, just as Arthur Schlesinger and John William Ward provide a context for Emerson, Thoreau, and Alcott. The literary artist must have that same sense of historical awareness that the historian seeks, or he, too, is incomplete.

There is, finally, a third level of relationship between history and literature arising from the fact that both involve the creative act. Something exists, after the historian and the literary artist have been at work, that has not existed before—an insight into human motivation, a metaphor that adds meaning to experience, a reason for an event, a perception of a relationship, a cause for an effect. Something has been done with and to the materials with which literature and history work; they have been related in a new way, formed into a new construct, articulated into a new statement.

Both historian and literary artist begin with the "fact" (however we define that term), with the raw material from which the creative process starts and out of which it shapes something new. Yet it is clear that the "facts" and materials with which the historian and literary artist deal are not the same in kind or quality. A historical fact is an actual past event, tied to a particular plane of reality; it happened, and it cannot be changed. The historian cannot move beyond his definition of history as past ac-

145

tion; he is confined always by the past, and always by actuality. The fact with which he deals is never contemporary, for it contains a built-in, instant evanescence; to the historian all the things with which he works are immediately recessive in time. A literary fact is an imaginative event; but it is no less usable or real for all of that. We know that Stephen Crane was too young to have served in the Civil War, that Walt Whitman never had by any means all the experiences he claimed to have had, that Mark Twain cheerfully "stretched the truth" as he called it; but this made no difference, ultimately, in the reality of what they wrote.

This problem of "pastness" is peculiarly the historian's limitation. He must deal always with an event that is forever gone, that survives only as memory or record, neither of which is the event itself. The problem of history is its temporality; the facts with which it deals are constantly being annihilated. The situation, as Jean Paul Sartre once remarked, is something like sitting in a speeding automobile, facing backward, so that the present instant is always just past. The literary artist, of course, has this problem too, but he can solve it by certain kinds of creative reconstruction denied the historian. Consider the case of Marcel Proust, who conceived the artist's role as the retrieval and recapitulation of the past, much as

any historian might. His aim was to recreate a culture
and a society so completely through memory that they
would remain forever untouched by temporality—the
sound of a street vendor's cry in the Paris of 1890, the
taste of tea, the rattle of a passing cart, the rustle of the
skirt of a long-dead girl, the look of wallpaper in a
vanished room. The problem of the artist, he wrote in
The Past Recaptured,

is to rediscover, to grasp again, and lay before us that
reality from which we have so far removed . . . . , to grasp
again our life, and also the life of others.

Yet Proust was not a historian, obviously, nor was
his reconstruction of his vanished Paris one that the
historian can fully accept as reality. Proust's success
was imaginative, not historical, and his defeat of time
symbolic rather than actual.

What the artist tries to find in his treatment of the
past, as Proust did, is the relation of the individual to
his present experience, in the context of his relation
to the past experience of others. Like Proust, William
Faulkner infused his work too with this theme of
man's struggle against time. There is in *Intruder in
the Dust* a magnificent passage in which Faulkner
probes into the mind of a young and sensitive Southern boy who muses on the stream of the past that lies
behind him:

147

It's all *now* you see. Yesterday won't be over until tomorrow and tomorrow began ten thousand years ago. For every Southern boy fourteen years old, not once but whenever he wants it, there is the instant when it's still not yet two o'clock on that July afternoon in 1863, the brigades are in position behind the rail fence, the guns are laid and ready in the woods and the furled flags are already loosened to break out and Pickett himself with his long oiled ringlets and his hat in one hand probably and his sword in the other looking up the hill waiting for Longstreet to give the word and it's all in the balance, it hasn't happened yet, it hasn't even begun yet but there is still time for it not to begin against that position and those circumstances which made more men than Garnett and Kemper and Armistead and Wilcox look grave yet it's going to begin, we all know that, we have come too far with too much at stake and that moment doesn't need even a fourteen-year old boy to think *This time Maybe this time.* . . .

The literary artist can handle this problem of pastness in ways that the historian cannot. As Faulkner once said of his characters, "I can move these people around like God, not only in space, but in time. . . . There is no such thing as *was*, only *is*." No historian, obviously, could say this, for the past tense is the only one in which he is allowed to operate. He has only to work with what has actually happened, or as close to it as he can; the novelist or the poet can work with what did not, or might have, or should have happened. The two must therefore approach reality differently. The rules of the historian's game bar him from doing what the poet or novelist, or even the biographer, is

148

allowed to do. The artist is permitted to deal with the *internal* currents of men's minds, with the emotions and ideas and motives that run beneath the masks that men assume. It is in removing the mask, in penetrating downward into the well of the individual consciousness that the Faulkners and Conrads and Eliots and Robert Lowells find their true purposes.

The poet and the novelist begin with a special situation. The reader agrees to what the critics have called a "willing suspension of disbelief"; that is, he expects to find a different kind of reality, knowing that what he is about to read is imaginative. With this attitude at work for him in the mind of the reader, the literary artist can make what he writes seem present, here and now—the *is* rather than the *was*, as Faulkner suggested.

The historian begins with no such concessions; for the reader will not, for him, suspend the normal sense of human temporality. The historian must deal with externals; he is always subject to iron laws of chronology and authenticity. The shadowy, internal world open to the literary artist, where time and proof need not exist, is closed to him. Yet this does not mean that the historian's world is not one equally exacting or exciting. The historian has the possibility of creating—and the word is an accurate one in this context—a world that is as close to actuality as his skill and industry can make it. To establish the record of what

149

men have done and said and thought, is an essential requisite to an understanding of the human condition, an accomplishment as indispensable to man's realization of himself and his world as anything the literary artist, operating under his less confining rules, may hope to do.

This is, then, the major difference between literature and history—that is, the differences of the *quality* of that reality which both seek to create. Robert Penn Warren, speaking in the Preface to his dramatic poem *Brother to Dragons* (1953), tried to define this important difference. His narrative is based on the family history of Thomas Jefferson's sister, who married Dr. Charles Lewis and moved to Kentucky; but Warren was well aware that he was not writing history:

> I am trying to write a poem and not a history, and therefore have no compunction about tampering with facts. But poetry is more than fantasy and is committed to the obligation of trying to say something about the human condition. Therefore a poem dealing with history is no more at liberty to violate what the writer takes to be the nature of the human heart. What he takes these things to be is, of course, his ultimate gamble.

Warren's novels provide exceptionally good examples of how the literary artist tries to answer the problem of reality. He has often based his novels on actual historical events, as he did his Pulitzer Prize novel of 1947, *All the King's Men*, which was presumably drawn from the career of Huey Long. Warren was praised and cursed for what many of his readers assumed was a thinly-disguised historical novel, which Warren protested it was not. In the 1953 edition of the novel, he remarked on this charge in his Preface, and what he wrote gives us an insight into the relationship between historical events and literary experience. Was Long the model for Willy Stark, the politician of the novel? Warren wrote:

I do not mean to imply that there was no connection between Governor Stark and Senator Long. Certainly it was the career of Long and the atmosphere of Louisiana that suggested the play that was to become the novel. But suggestion does not mean identity. . . . I did have some notions about the phenomenon of which Long was but one example, and I tried to put some of those notions into my book. . . . The book, however, was never intended to be a book about politics. Politics merely provided the framework story in which the deeper concerns, whatever their final significance, might work themselves out.[14]

Warren's statement is of great importance for our understanding of the literary attitude, as opposed to the historical, as it confronts the materials of experience. The true artist does more than use history; he

14. For a further analysis of the historical roots of the novel, see Warren's "*All the King's Men:* The Matrix of Experience," *Yale Review*, LIII (December, 1963), 161–67.

absorbs it. He assimilates the literal, factual, temporal world into the imaginative; the reality of the past is for him the base from which to speculate about those "deeper concerns" and "final significances"—as Warren calls them—of the human condition. What Warren speaks of is the difference between writing that is rearranged history, and that which is literature, or experience transmuted—the difference between the novels of William Faulkner and Kenneth Roberts, between Robert Lowell's *For the Union Dead* and Stephen Vincent Benét's *John Brown's Body*, between Melville's *Moby-Dick* and Richard Henry Dana's *Two Years before the Mast.*

In dealing with the materials of experience, both history and literature are concerned with human actions, passions, motives, and conduct so complex and variable that they cannot be precisely measured, predicted, or manipulated. As Albert Bushnell Hart once wrote of his craft, in words that could apply equally to his contemporary, Henry James:

We deal with manifold manifestations of human nature; we are trying to decipher triple and quadruple palimpsests of human character; to understand and to expound the actions of men who did not understand themselves.[15]

15. "Imagination in History," *American Historical Review,* **XV** (January, 1910), 234.

Literature and history ask the same questions about human nature. Their ultimate aim is to provide man with knowledge of himself by knowing what men have been and done,—and, hopefully, perhaps why. We know Burr challenged Hamilton, and that Hamilton accepted, and that Burr killed him. These things are fixed and accurate in time, place, and sequence. How are we to know what lay beneath—why Burr challenged, why Hamilton believed he must accept? How can we know what really is important for us to know in this episode of which we know all the facts, an episode of such great significance in determining the course of what happened after? The list of possibilities is endless—the first day at Gettysburg, the trial of Sacco and Vanzetti, the events at Ford's Theater or Dallas. At this point Ranke's belief that he, or anyone, could "tell you how it was" loses all meaning.

And it is also at this point that we have, I think, the highest and the most intimate relationship between history and literature: their concern with the relevance and the meaning of experience. "I would define history," writes English historian Geoffrey Barraclough,

as the attempt to discover, on the basis of fragmentary evidence, the significant things about the past and significant means significant now. The past, no doubt, existed for itself; but history exists for us. In other words, it should

153

be relevant to our needs, and provide answers for questions which concern us.[16]

Literature too exists for us, relevant to our needs, concerned with the questions to which each generation needs answers. This is the real meaning of the creative act common to both history and literature, an act that is fundamentally one of imagination.

This brings me to my final point, that history and literature, in perceiving the meanings of experience, are essentially imaginative; and that it is this common factor that makes an art of them both. The imagination, for the historian, performs two vital functions. The first of these is selection. The historian is not a camera; he cannot include all the facts for he cannot know them all. and even those that he knows are not all of equal value. The facts that the historian uses do not choose themselves; he selects them, orders them within some larger context. Facts, as the saying goes, do not speak for themselves; they say something only when chosen, arranged, and interpreted. Nor is the selective choice of the historian concerned only with facts. He must also choose the point at which he enters and leaves the stream of time and in thus giving his narrative a beginning and an end, he imposes a pattern on the historical past. History never stops; the historian has to stop it somewhere.

16. "The Relevance of History," *Books*, VI (March-April, 1960), 41–46.

The act of selection is essentially imaginative. It is an act the literary artist and the historian alike perform, for in making their choices out of the vast available territory of human experience they give shape and system to events—real or imagined. The selective decisions each makes determine the nature of the product each creates; the decisions themselves are basically imaginative, for there is no other guide.

If the first function of the imagination in history and literature is selective, the second is interpretative. This is the essence of both—the one brings order and meaning to the past, the other brings them to an experience beyond reality. History and literature are concerned with sequences of effects and causes, woven together in a complex tangle of relationships. What the historian or the literary artist knows about this web of events is never complete, and the information he receives never comes in a coherent pattern. What meaning he makes of it must come from the imagination. This is the creative act that relates the poet and the historian—the imaginative perception of meanings and relevancies each draws from his observations of human experience. There are differences in materials, of course, that limit each. The historian accumulates facts of a kind the poet does not, nor can his imagination operate in quite the same way as, say, the novelist's. The artist may mix real with imaginary events, so long as he stays within the boundaries of the probabilities of human behavior. Shakespeare, in creating a Caesar or a Macbeth, may select and combine and invent within elastic limits not granted to the historian. Hamlet needs no birth certificate, but Napoleon does.

While we require from both the historian and the literary artist this creative act of imagination, we demand of the historian additional tests of the validity of his view of what things mean. We place him under a handicap, quite deliberately, and shackle him to more exacting proofs. The Italian historian Gaetano Salvimini furnished a good illustration of how this is done. Suppose, he said, that we excavate a Roman statue with a missing head. The archaeologist and the historian agree that the head must have worn a helmet, perhaps even of a particular design, and demonstrate proof of this in various ways—by reference to other statues of the period, from contemporary sculptors' styles, from detailed knowledge of Roman military accoutrements. But at this point the historical imagination must stop, while the artistic imagination may continue. The sculptor who recreates the missing head has much greater freedom in visualizing and executing it; he must respect the style of the historical period in which it existed, of course, but the face of the statue he may see as he wishes. Two sculptors, in fact, might provide two quite different faces for it without violating the rules of credibility. Thus the historical and the artistic imagination, whose functions may be much the same, must operate under different conditions.

I do not mean to imply that these restrictions need be disabling to the historian; they intensify his task, and may even be advantageous. The imagination, for the historian as well as the literary artist, has a number of vital purposes. It serves as the power of invention, the judge of hypotheses and theories; it discerns beginnings and causes, as well as conclusions. It allows the historian to perceive the significance of facts, to penetrate into and beneath them. Good historical writing, I believe, is under constant tension, with the imagination always pushing outward against the restraining discipline of historical plausibility. There is always in history this contest between what the imagination wants to say and the rules of fact and temporality that restrict it. The literary artist has boundaries as well to his imagination, and the highest form of literature is infused with this same tensile quality. But there are limits beyond which the historian has no right to go, a territory of the imagination into which the literary artist may penetrate, but denied to his compatriot. George Kennan has explained this very well:

It is precisely in resisting the temptation to go further that his quality as a historian, as distinct from a literary person

157

pure and simple, is most basically expressed. The true mark
of his trade is that he accepts a set of rules far more rigorous and confining than those which govern the novelist or
the poet. He cannot create the pieces of his puzzle; he must
attempt to put it together from those he finds lying around.
No only that, but having found a few pieces, he cannot even
order them to his heart's desire. They are ordered for him
chronologically in advance by that most imperious of all
historical masters, the documented date, and before this
authority he must bow his head in unquestioning obe-
dience. . . .[17]

The historian may begin his task as an objective,
impartial observer, following all the rules of evidence,
weighing the facts and presenting them without dis-
tortion or preconception; but before he is through, he
is bound to find himself doing what the literary artist
does, and for much the same reasons—that is, giving
a view of life, an estimate of the human condition,
a perspective on the world we have lived in, a judgment on the success or failure of man's aspirations.
He cannot help it, for he is dealing with human
beings, with their ideas and beliefs, with things derived from the hearts and minds of men long gone
but whose minds and hearts once were quick and
sensitive. Like the literary artist, he is looking for
what was real in life and the records of life. These

17. *New York Times Book Review,* April 26, 1959. © 1959 by
the New York Times Company. Reprinted by permission. For an interesting discussion of the use of the historical imagination in a reconstruction based on limited and final evidence, see William Bradley,
"The Quest of the Historical Jesus," *Journal of Religion,* XLV (January, 1963), 35–47.

things are implicit in the past, and the historian, because he interprets the past, cannot help but illuminate it by his search. "The historian, in other words," Bruce Catton recently wrote, "in spite of himself, is in literature, and there is no earthly way to keep him out of it." [18]

The excitement of history and of literature, and their significance as art, lies in that risk mentioned by Kennan, in the gamble they are willing to take in coming as close to their boundaries as they dare to go. It is in this, I believe, that they are art and not science—for science cannot gamble, and art must. The historian and the literary artist are bound by the same risks, related by the same liabilities, dependent on the same creative, imaginative powers. They must make their personal selections from what experience presents to them, hoping that their choices are valid; they must make judgments about the meanings of experience, hoping all the while that their judgments are useful; they must make final declarations about the values of experience, hoping all the while that their declarations are wise. History is an art, perhaps an art trying to be a science, but always an art, whether it succeeds or not. If by their fruits ye shall know them, history and literature are assuredly branches of the same tree.

18. See his address to the Society of American Historians, *History as Literature* (New York, 1964).

A Selected Bibliography

MARGARET E. KAHN AND
GEORGE P. SCHOYER

A Selected Bibliography of Books and Articles
on the Use of Literature in Research in
American History

I. GENERAL

ALDERFER, E. GORDON. "Some Traditions of Pennsylvania Literature," *Pennsylvania Library Notes*, XVII (1939), 7–14.

ARAGONNÈS, CLAUDE. "L'Américain et son passé," *La Table ronde*, No. 105, pp. 16–21.

ARNOLD, AEROL. "Why Structure in Fiction: A Note to Social Scientists," *American Quarterly*, X (1958), 325–37.

BINNS, JOHN H. "Northwest Region: Fact or Fiction?" *Pacific Northwest Quarterly*, XLVIII (1957), 65–75.

BLANKENSHIP, RUSSELL. *American Literature as an Expression of the National Mind*. New York: Holt, 1931.

BLOTNER, JOSEPH. *The Political Novel*. Garden City, N. Y.: Doubleday, 1955.

BOWRON, BERNARD; LEO MARX; and ARNOLD ROSE. "Literature and Covert Culture," in *Studies in American Culture*, ed. JOSEPH KWIAT and MARY TURPIE. Minneapolis: University of Minnesota Press, 1960.

BOYNTON, PERCY. *Literature and American Life*. New York: Ginn, 1936.

———. *The Rediscovery of the Frontier*. Chicago: University of Chicago Press, 1931.

BROWN, STERLING A. *The Negro in American Fiction*. Washington, D. C.: Associates in Negro Folk Education, 1937.

A SELECTED BIBLIOGRAPHY

BUTCHER, MARGARET JUST. *The Negro in American Culture.* Based on materials left by ALAIN LOCKE. New York: Knopf, 1956.

CLARK, EDWARD. "Images of the Negro in the American Novel," *Jahrbuch für Amerikastudien,* V (1960), 175–84.

CLARK, H. H. "Nationalism in American Literature," *University of Toronto Quarterly,* II (1933), 491–515.

DERLETH, AUGUST. "On the Use of Local History in Fiction," *Wisconsin Magazine of History,* XLI (1958), 79–84.

DEVOTO, BERNARD. "Interrelations of History and Literature," in *Approaches to American Social History,* ed. WILLIAM LINGLEBACH. New York: Appleton Century, 1937.

DONDORE, DOROTHY. "Early Romantic Treatments," "The Realism of the Mississippi Valley," "Recent Tendencies," and "Romantic Treatments after 1870," in *The Prairie and the Making of Middle America: Four Centuries of Description.* Cedar Rapids, Ia: The Torch Press, 1926.

———. "Points of Contact between History and Literature in the Mississippi Valley," *Mississippi Valley Historical Review,* XI (1924-25), 227–36.

EGBERT, DONALD DREW, and STOW PERSONS (eds.). *Socialism and American Life.* With a Bibliography by T. D. SEYMOUR BASSETT. Princeton: Princeton University Press, 1952, II, 421–510.

FLORY, CLAUDE R. *Economic Criticism in American Fiction, 1792-1900.* Philadelphia: University of Pennsylvania Press, 1936.

GOODWYN, FRANK. "The Frontier in American Fiction," *Inter-American Review of Bibliography,* X (1960), 356–59.

A SELECTED BIBLIOGRAPHY

HAZARD, LUCY. *The Frontier in American Life*. New York: Thomas Y. Crowell, 1927.

HERRON, I. H. *The Small Town in American Literature*. Durham, N. C.: Duke University Press, 1939.

HOFFMAN, FREDERICK J. "The Knowledge of Literature: Suggestions for American Studies," *American Quarterly*, X (Summer, 1958), 199–205.

HUBBELL, JAY. *Southern Life in Fiction*. Athens: University of Georgia Press, 1960.

JONES, HOWARD MUMFORD. "American Literature and the Melting Pot," *"Southeast Review*, XXXVI (1940–41), 329–46.

———. "American Literature as an Instrument for Cultural Analysis," in *Ideas in America*. Cambridge: Harvard University Press, 1944.

———. "Fifty Guides to American Literature," *Saturday Review of Literature*, XXIX (October 12, 1946), 15–16, 57.

———. *The Frontier in American Fiction*. Jerusalem: Hebrew University, 1956.

KANTOR, MACKINLAY. "The Historical Novelist's Obligation to History," *Iowa Journal of History*, LIX (1962), 27–44.

KEISER, ALBERT. *The Indian in American Literature*. New York: Oxford University Press, 1933.

KENNAN, GEORGE F. "It's History, but Is It Literature?" *New York Times Book Review*, April 29, 1959, pp. 1, 34–35.

KWIAT, JOSEPH and MARY TURPIE (eds.). *Studies in American Culture*. Minneapolis: University of Minnesota Press, 1960.

165

MIZENER, ARTHUR M. "The Thin Intelligent Face of American Fiction," *Kenyon Review*, XVII (1955), 507–24.

MONROE, NELLIE. *The Novel and Society*. Chapel Hill: University of North Carolina Press, 1941.

MORISON, SAMUEL ELIOT. "History as a Literary Art," in *By Land and by Sea: Essays and Addresses*. New York: Alfred A. Knopf, 1953.

NELSON, J, H, *The Negro Character in American Literature*. Lawrence: University of Kansas Press, 1926.

NEVINS, ALLAN. "Literary Aspects of History," in *Gateway to History*. Chicago: D. C. Heath, 1938.

NICHOLS, CHARLES. "Color, Conscience and Crucifixion: A Study of Racial Attitudes in American Literature and Criticism," *Jahrbuch für Amerikastudien*, VI (1961), 37-47.

O'CONNOR, WILLIAM VAN. "The Novel and the 'Truth' about America," in *Studies in American Culture*, ed. JOSEPH KWIAT and MARY TURPIE. Minneapolis: University of Minnesota Press, 1960.

———. "The Novel as a Social Document," *American Quarterly*, IV (1952), 169–75.

PEARCE, ROY HARVEY. "Literature, History and Humanism: An Americanist's Dilemma," *College English*, XXIV (1963), 364–72.

REDDING, JAY SAUNDERS. *To Make a Poet Black*. Chapel Hill: University of North Carolina Press, 1939.

ROOSEVELT, THEODORE. *History as Literature, and Other Essays*. New York: Charles Scribner's Sons, 1913.

RUDOLPH, EARLE LEIGHTON. "The Frontier in American Literature," *Jahrbuch für Amerikastudien*, VII (1962), 77–91.

SCHLESINGER, ARTHUR M. "Social History in American Literature," *Yale Review*, XVIII (1928), 135–47.

SILLARS, MALCOM O. "Warren's *All the King's Men*: A Study in Populism," *American Quarterly*, IX (1957), 345–53.

SMITH, HENRY NASH. *Virgin Land: The American West as Symbol and Myth*. Cambridge: Harvard University Press, 1950.

SMITH, REBECCA. "Portrait of an American: The National Character in Fiction," *Southwest Review*, XXI (1936), 245–60.

SONNICHSEN, C. L. (ed.). *The Southwest in Life and Literature*. New York: Devin-Adair, 1962.

STECKMESSER, KENT L. "The Frontier Hero in History and Legend," *Wisconsin Magazine of History*, XLVI (1963), 168–79.

STEUBER, WILLIAM F., JR., "Using History for Fiction," *Wisconsin Magazine of History*, XLIII (1960), 245–52.

TAYLOR, WALTER. *The Economic Novel in America*. Chapel Hill: University of North Carolina Press, 1942.

WALSH, WARREN B. "Is History a Science?" in *Perspectives and Patterns*. Syracuse: Syracuse University Press, 1962.

II. BEFORE 1865

BASLER, ROY P. "Lincoln in Literature," *Illinois State Historical Society Journal*, LII (1959), 33–34.

BLACK, ALBERT. "The Pontiac Conspiracy in the Novel, 1833–1954," *Michigan History*, XLIII (1959), 115–19.

BLAYNEY, GLEN H. "City Life in American Drama, 1825–1860," in *Studies in Honor of John Wilcox*, eds. WALLACE A. DOYLE and WOODBURN O. ROSS. Detroit: Wayne State University Press, 1958.

BOHNER, CHARLES H. *"Swallow Barn:* John P. Kennedy's Chronicle of Virginia Society," *Virginia Magazine of History and Biography*, LXVIII (1960), 317–30.

BROOKS, CHARLES. *Puritanism in New England Fiction, 1820–1870*. Princeton, N. J.: Princeton University Press, 1943.

CARDWELL, GUY A. "The Idea of Progress North and South: 1860," *Georgia Review*, XI (1957), 271–78.

CELVILLE, DEREK. "History and Humor: The Tall Tale in New Orleans," *Louisiana Historical Quarterly*, XXXIX (1956), 153–67.

DAVIS, LEONA. "Literary Opinions on Slavery in American Literature from after the American Revolution to the Civil War," *Negro History Bulletin*, XXIII (1960), 99–101, 104, 123–27, 147–50.

DICKINSON, LEON T. "Civil War Humor: Its Role in Novels on Slavery," *Civil War History*, II (1956), 49–65.

DOUBLEDAY, NEAL. "Hawthorne's Criticism of New England Life," *College English*, II (1941), 639–53.

EBY, CECIL D., JR. " 'The Real War' and the Books," *Southwest Review* XLVII (1962), 259–64.

FUSSEL, EDWIN. *Frontier: American Literature and the American West*. Princeton, N. J.: Princeton University Press, 1965.

GROSS, SEYMOUR L. "Hawthorne's 'My Kinsman, Major Molineux': History as Moral Adventure," *Nineteenth-Century Fiction*, XII (1957), 97–109.

168

HANCHETT, WILLIAM. "Civil War History—from Poetry," *Western Humanities Review,* XVI (1962), 257–71.

HARDING, WALTER. "American History in the Novel: The Period of Expansion, 1815–1861," *Midwest Journal,* VIII (1965), 393–98.

HILL, LAWRENCE. *Hawthorne: Critic of Society.* New Haven, Conn.: Yale University Press, 1944.

HUBBELL, JAY. "Cavalier and Indentured Servant in Virginia Fiction," *South Atlantic Quarterly,* XXVI (1927), 22–39.

HUBBELL, JAY B. "The Smith-Pocahontas Story in Literature," *Virginia Magazine of History and Biography,* LXV (1957), 275–300.

HUNGERFORD, HAROLD R. "That Was at Chancellorsville: The Factual Framework of *The Red Badge of Courage,*" *American Literature,* XXXIV (1963), 520–31.

LIVELY, ROBERT. *Fiction Fights the Civil War.* Chapel Hill: University of North Carolina Press, 1957.

McDOWELL, TREMAINE. "The Negro in the Southern Novel Prior to 1850," *Journal of English and German Philology,* XXV (1926), 455–73.

MARTIN, TERENCE. "Social Institutions in the Early American Novel," *American Quarterly,* IX (1957), 72–84.

MURDOCK, KENNETH. "The Colonial Experience in the Literature of the U.S.," *American Philosophical Society Proceedings,* C (1956), 129–32.

ORIANS, G. HARRISON. "Cannon through the Forest: Novels of the Land Battles of the War of 1812 in the Old Northwest," *Ohio History,* LXXII (1963), 195–219.

———. "New England Witchcraft in Fiction," *American Literature,* II (1930), 54–71.

————. "Pontiac in Literature: Part I, 1764–1915," *Northwest Ohio Quarterly*, XXXV (1963), 144–63.

PHILLIPS, WILLIAM. "American History in the Novel: The Colonial Period, 1585–1775," *Midwest Journal*, VIII (1956), 376–84.

RAGAN, JAMES F. "Hawthorne's Bulky Puritans," *PMLA*, LXXV (1960), 420–23.

ROSS, JOHN. *The Social Criticism of Fenimore Cooper.* Berkeley: University of California Press, 1933.

RUBIN, LOUIS D., JR. "The Image of an Army: Southern Novelists and the Civil War," *Texas Quarterly*, I (1958) 17–34.

RUSSELL, JASON. "Cooper: Interpreter of the Real and the Historical Indian," *Journal of American History*, XXIII (1930), 41–71.

STAFFORD, JOHN. *The Literary Criticism of "Young America": A Study in the Relationship of Politics and Literature, 1837–1850.* Berkeley: University of California Press, 1952.

STONE, ALBERT E., JR. "Reading, Writing, and History: Best Novel of the Civil War," *American Heritage*, XIII (1962), 84–88.

TANDY, JEANNETTE, R. "Pro-Slavery Propaganda in American Fiction of the Fifties," *South Atlantic Quarterly*, XXI (1922), 41–50, 170–78.

THOMPSON, LAWRENCE S. "The Civil War in Fiction," *Civil War History*, II (1956), 83–95.

TURNER, LORENZO. *Anti-Slavery Sentiment in American Literature prior to 1865.* Washington, D.C.: Association for the Study of Negro Life and History, 1929.

WEATHERS, WILLIE T., "Moby Dick and the Nineteenth-Century Scene," *Texas Studies in Literature and Language,* I (1960), 477–501.

WILSON, EDMUND. *Patriotic Gore: Studies in the Literature of the American Civil War.* New York: Oxford University Press, 1962.

WOODRESS, JAMES. "American History in the Novel: The Revolution and Early National Periods, 1775–1815," *Midwest Journal,* VIII (1956), 385–92.

WRIGHT, THOMAS. *Literary Culture in Early New England, 1620–1730.* New Haven: Yale University Press, 1920.

III. AFTER 1865

AARON, DANIEL. *Writers on the Left.* New York: Harcourt, Brace, 1961.

———. "Self or Society?" *New York Times Book Review,* February 14, 1965, pp. 1, 37–39.

ARDEN, EUGENE. "The Early Harlem Novel," *Phylon Quarterly,* XX (1959), 25–31.

AUBERG, PIERRE. "Les 'Industrial Workers of the World' dans l'œuvre de Sinclair Lewis," *Revue socialiste,* No. 99 (1956), 178–97.

BADER, ARNO L. "Melodrama in Ohio: Avery Hopwood and Boss Cox of Cincinnati," *Ohio History Quarterly,* LXX (1961), 145–51.

BANKS, LOY OTIS. "The Credible Literary West," *Colorado Quarterly,* VIII (1959), 28–50.

BASS, ALTHA "The Social Consciousness of William Dean Howells," *New Republic,* XXVI (1921), 192–94.

BAXTER, ANNETTE K. "Caste and Class: Howells' Boston and Wharton's New York," *Midwest Quarterly,* IV (1963), 353–61.

BECK, RICHARD. "Rolvaag, Interpreter of Immigrant Life," *North Dakota Quarterly,* XXIV (Winter, 1956), 26–36.

BECKER, ALLEN W. "Ellen Glasgow's Social History," *University of Texas Studies in English,* XXXVI (1957), 12–19.

BLAKE, NELSON MANFRED. "How to Learn History from Sinclair Lewis and Other Uncommon Sources," *Stetson University Bulletin,* LXIV (July, 1964), 1–17.

BLOOMFIELD, MAXWELL. "Dixon's *The Leopard's Spots*: A Study in Popular Racism," *American Quarterly,* XVI (1964), 387–401.

BODE, CARL. "Lloyd Douglas: Loud Voice in the Wilderness," *American Quarterly,* II (1950), 340–52.

BREMNER, ROBERT H. *From the Depths: The Discovery of Poverty in the United States.* New York: New York University Press, 1956. Pp. 87–107, 164–84.

BRUNING, EBERHARD. "The Spanish Civil War (1936–1939) and the American Novel," *Zeitschrift für Anglistik und Amerikanistik,* XI (1963), 42–55.

CASSADY, EDWARD E. "Muckraking in the Gilded Age," *American Literature,* XIII (1941–42), 134–41.

CAWELTI, JOHN G. "Changing Ideas of Social Reform as Seen in Selected American Novels of the 1850's, the

1880's, and the Present Day," *Social Service Review,* XXXV (1961), 278–89.

CHASE, MARY ELLEN. "Sarah Orne Jewett as a Social Historian," *Prairie Schooner,* XXXVI (1962), 231–37.

CURTI, MERLE. "Dime Novels and the American Tradition," *Yale Review,* XXVI (1937), 761–78.

DANIELS, R. BALFOUR. "George Ade as Social Critic," *Mississippi Quarterly,* XII (1959), 194–204.

DAVIES, WALLACE EVAN. "Religious Issues in Late Nineteenth-Century American Novels," *Bulletin of the John Rylands Library,* XLI (1959), 328–59.

DAVIS, ARTHUR. "Integration and Race Literature," *Phylon,* XVII (1956), 141–46.

DeVoto, BERNARD. *The Literary Fallacy.* Boston: Little, Brown, 1944.

FONER, PHILIP S. *Mark Twain: Social Critic.* New York: International Publishers, 1958.

FORD, NICK. *The Contemporary Negro Novel: A Study in Race Relations.* Boston: Meador Publishing Co., 1936.

FOSTER, RICHARD. "The Contemporaneity of Howells," *New England Quarterly,* XXXII (1959), 54–78.

FREDERICK, JOHN T. "Fiction of the Second World War," *College English,* XVII (1956), 197–204; *English Journal,* XLIV (1955), 451–58.

GLICKENSBERG, CHARLES. "Negro Fiction in America," *South Atlantic Quarterly,* XLV (1946), 477–88.

GLOSTER, HUGH. *Negro Voices in American Fiction.* Chapel Hill: University of North Carolina Press, 1948.

GOODWIN, GEORGE, JR. "The Last Hurrahs: George Apley and Frank Skeffington," *Massachusetts Review,* I (1960), 461–71.

GRIMES, ALAN, and JANET OWEN. "Civil Rights and the Race Novel," *Chicago Jewish Forum,* XV (1956), 12–15.

GROSS, THEODORE. "The Negro in the Literature of Reconstruction," *Phylon,* XXII (1961), 5–14.

GROSS, THEODORE L. "The South in the Literature of Reconstruction," *Mississippi Quarterly,* XIV (1961), 68–78.

GUTTMAN, ALLEN, "Mechanized Doom: Ernest Hemingway and the Spanish Civil War," *Massachusetts Review,* I (1960), 541–61.

HARRINGTON, FRED. "Literary Aspects of American Anti-Imperialism, 1898–1902," *New England Quarterly,* X (1947), 650–67.

HARVEY, CHARLES. "The Dime Novel in American Life," *Atlantic Monthly,* C (1907), 37–45.

HICKS, GRANVILLE. "What to Be after Poughkeepsie," *Saturday Review of Literature,* XLVI (August 31, 1963), 27–28.

HIMELSTEIN, MORGAN Y. *Drama Was a Weapon: The Left-Wing Theatre in New York, 1929–1941.* New Brunswick, N. J.: Rutgers University Press, 1963.

HOFSTADTER, RICHARD and BEATRICE. "Winston Churchill: A Study of the Popular Novel," *American Quarterly,* II (1950), 12–28.

IRWIN, WILLIAM. "Dos Passos and Fitzgerald as Reviewers of the Social Scene," *Die Neueren Sprachen,* IX (1960), 417–28.

JOHNSON, GEORGE W. "The Frontier behind Frank Norris's *McTeague,*" *Huntington Library Quarterly,* XXVI (1962), 91–104.

KAHN, LOTHAR. "The Jewish Soldier in Modern Fiction," *American Judaism,* IX (1960), 12–13, 30–31.

KAPLAN, CHARLES. "American History in the Novel: The Period of Development, 1861–1900," *Midwest Journal,* VIII (1956), 397–406.

KAZIN, ALFRED. "The Historian as Reporter: Edmund Wilson and the 1930's," *Reporter,* XVIII (March 20, 1958), 43–46.

KOERNER, J. D. "The Last of the Muckrake Men," *South Atlantic Quarterly,* LV (1956), 221–32.

LÉTARGEZ, J. "Robert Penn Warren's Views of History," *Revue des langues vivantes,* XXII (1956), 533–43.

LEWIS, MARVIN. "A Free Life in the Mines and on the Range," *Western Humanities Review,* XII (1958), 87–95.

LITTLEFIELD, HENRY. "The Wizard of Oz: Parable on Populism," *American Quarterly,* XVI (1964), 47–58.

McCORMICK, JOHN. "The Novel and Society," *Jahrbuch für Amerikastudien,* I (1956), 70–75.

MACLACHEN, JOHN. "Folk and Culture in the Novels of Erskine Caldwell," *Southern Folklore Quarterly,* IX (1945), 93–101.

175

MEYER, ROY W. *The Middle Western Farm Novel in the Twentieth Century.* Lincoln: University of Nebraska Press, 1965.

———. "The Scandinavian Immigrant in American Farm Fiction," *American Scandinavian Review,* LXVII (1959), 248–49.

MOERS, ELLEN. "Teddy Roosevelt: Literary Feller," *Columbia University Forum,* VI (Summer, 1963), 10–16.

NELSON, LAWRENCE W. "Mary Johnston and the Historic Imagination," in *The Dilemma of the Southern Writer,* ed. RICHARD K. MEEKER. Farmville, Va.: Longwood College, 1961.

NOBLE, DAVID. "Dreiser and Veblen and the Literature of Social Change," in *Studies in American Culture,* ed. JOSEPH KWIAT and MARY TURPIE. Minneapolis: University of Minnesota Press, 1960.

OLSEN, OTTO H. *Carpetbaggers' Crusade: The Life of Albion Tourgee.* Baltimore: Johns Hopkins Press, 1965. Pp. 223–41.

OSTERWEIS, ROLLIN G. "The Problems of Literary Biography in Relation to American Jewish History," *Publications of the American Jewish Historical Association,* XLVI (1957), 426–32.

PILKINGTON, JOHN. "History and Literature in Mississippi since 1900," *Journal of Mississippi History,* XX (1958), 234–43.

PODHORETZ, NORMAN. "Gibbsville and New Leeds: The America of John O'Hara and Mary McCarthy," *Commentary,* XXI (1956), 269–73.

RIDEOUT, WALTER. "O Workers' Revolution . . . the True Messiah: The Jew as Author and Subject in the American Radical Novel," *American Jewish Archives*, XI (1959), 157–75.

———. *The Radical Novel in the United States, 1900–1954.* Cambridge, Mass.: Harvard University Press, 1956.

ROSE, LISLE ABBOTT. "A Bibliographical Survey of Economic and Political Writings, 1865–1900," *American Literature*, XV (1943–44), 381–410.

SANFORD, CHARLES. "Classics of American Reform Literature," *American Quarterly*, X (1958), 295–311.

SCHNEIDER, ROBERT W. *Five Novelists of the Progressive Era.* New York: Columbia University Press, 1966.

SPEARS, MORRIS. *The Political Novel.* New York: Oxford University Press, 1924.

STEINBERG, ABRAHAM H. "Jewish Characters in Fugitive American Novels of the Nineteenth Century," *Yivo Annual of Jewish Social Sciences*, XI (1956–57), 105–21.

STRUGNELL, JOHN R. "Robert Penn Warren and the Uses of the Past," *Review of English Literature*, IV (1963), 93–102.

TITUS, WARREN I. "The Progressivism of the Muckrakers: A Myth Re-examined through Fiction," *Journal of the Central Mississippi Valley American Studies Association*, I (1960), 10–16.

WALKER, ROBERT. "The Poet and the Rise of the City," *Mississippi Valley Historical Review*, XLIX (1962), 85–99.

177

———. "The Poet and the Robber Baron," *American Quarterly*, XIII (1961), 447–65.

———. "The Poets Interpret the Western Frontier," *Mississippi Valley Historical Review*, XLVII (1961), 619–38.

WEISSBUCH, TED N. "Albion W. Tourgee: Propagandist and Critic of Reconstruction," *Ohio Historical Quarterly*, LXX (1961), 27–44.

WHITE, ELLINGTON. "Robert Penn Warren," in *South: Modern Southern Literature in Its Cultural Setting*, ed. LOUIS D. RUBIN and ROBERT D. JACOBS. Garden City, N. Y.: Doubleday, 1961.

WILSON, HOWARD. "The Historian's Mark Twain," *Social Studies*, XXVI (1935), 505–12.

WITHAM, W. TASKER. *The Adolescent in the American Novel: 1920–1960*. New York: Frederick Ungar, 1964.

WOODWARD, C. VANN. "The Historical Dimension," *Virginia Quarterly Review*, XXXII (1956), 258–67.

WRIGHT, LYLE H. "A Few Observations on American Fiction, 1851–1875," *Proceedings of the American Antiquarian Society*, LXV (1955), 75–104.

Notes on the Contributors

CONTRIBUTORS

DANIEL AARON is professor of English language and literature at Smith College. He is the author of *Writers on the Left* and *Men of Good Hope*.

ROBERT H. BREMNER is professor of history at the Ohio State University, and the author of *From the Depths: The Discovery of Poverty in the United States*.

MARGARET E. KAHN is assistant professor of library administration at the Ohio State University.

EDWARD LURIE, professor of history at Wayne State University, is the author *Louis Agassiz: A Life in Science*. Professors Aaron and Lurie are collaborating on a study of the impact of the Civil War on American literature and intellectual life.

RUSSEL B. NYE is professor of English at Michigan State University. His books include *The Cultural Life of the New Nation, Midwestern Progressive Politics,* and *George Bancroft, Brahmin Rebel*.

181

CONTRIBUTORS

STOW PERSONS, professor of history at the State University of Iowa, is the author of *American Minds* and the editor of *Evolutionary Thought in America.*

GEORGE P. SCHOYER is an instructor in library administration at the Ohio State University.

Index

INDEX

Abolitionism, 142
Adams, Charles Francis, 129
Adams, George B., 136
Adams, Henry, 35–44, 46–80 *passim*, 132, 136; as historian, 130–31; quoted on Federalists, 131
Adams, John, 113
Adams, John Quincy, 64
Addison, Joseph, 86
Agassiz, Alex, 79
Agassiz, Louis, 44, 45, 46, 51, 55–64, 72–73, 75, 80, 97
Alcott, Bronson, 145
Aldrich, Thomas Bailey, 98
Algren, Nelson, 18, 141
All the King's Men (Warren), 151
Ambassadors, The (James), 143
American, The (James), 143
American Historical Association, 126, 134, 136
"American Scholar, The" (Emerson), 143
Andrews, Charles McLean, 129
Aspern Papers, The (James), 12, 54
Astor, John Jacob, 99
Atlantic Monthly, 51, 73
Auden, W. H., 3
Austen, Jane, 86

Bache, Alexander Dallas, 44, 45, 46, 47, 72
Bancroft, George, 124, 125, 126, 127, 128, 129, 130, 137
Barraclough, Geoffrey, 153
Beard, Charles A., 31, 35, 54, 55, 66
Becker, Carl L., 137
Bell, Alexander Graham, 79
Benét, Stephen Vincent, 152
Beowulf, 141
Berkeley, George, 54
Boas, Franz, 79
Boston, Mass., 45, 68, 73, 86, 91, 96, 98, 141
Boston Quarterly Review, 123
Bourne, Randolph, 47, 71
Brother to Dragons (Warren), 150
Bryan, William Jennings, 39, 144
Bryant, William Cullen, 109
Bullock, Alan, 26
Burke, Kenneth, 22–23, 50
Burr, Aaron, 153
Byron, George Gordon, Lord, 110

Cambridge, Mass., 39, 45, 73, 77
Cameron, Elizabeth, 39
Carlyle, Thomas, 124
Catton, Bruce, 144, 159

Century Club (New York), 66
Channing, Edward, 136
Chatham, William Pitt, Lord, 86
Cheever, John, 141
Chesterfield, Philip Stanhope, Lord, 86
Churchill, Winston, 138
Civil War, 24, 107, 144, 146
Clark, George Rogers, 133
Coleridge, Samuel Taylor, 108
Concord, Mass., 107, 108
Conroy, Jack, 18
Cooper, James Fenimore, 85, 87, 90, 93, 101–2, 103–4, 109, 124
Cornell, Ezra, 65, 66
Cosmos Club (Washington, D.C.), 36, 41, 45, 66, 79
Cowley, Malcolm, 4 n.
Crane, Stephen, 78, 141, 144, 146
Crawford, Thomas, 99
Curtis, George William, 68, 91–92

Dana, Richard Henry, 152
Darwin, Charles, 69
"Darwinism," 69–70
Dell, Floyd, 4 n.
Democracy (Adams), 37
Dewey, John, 31, 34, 35, 54, 71, 78
Donnelly, Ignatius, 144
Dreiser, Theodore, 141
Dumas, Alexander, 130

Early Memories (Lodge), 38
Eastman, Max, 4 n.
Education of Henry Adams, The, x, 35–36, 37, 38, 50–51, 70, 75, 77, 130
Eliot, Charles William, 64, 65, 66, 67

Eliot, Samuel Atkins, 67
Eliot, T. S., 3, 149
Ely, Richard T., 78
Emerson, Ralph Waldo, 47, 58, 73, 84, 86, 89–90, 97, 102, 124, 125, 141, 143, 144, 145
Everett, Edward, 104, 105

Farrell, James T., 141
Faulkner, William, 141, 147–48, 149, 152
Fielding, Henry, 86
Fiske, John, 136
Fitzgerald, F. Scott, 141
For the Union Dead (Lowell), 152
Forbes, John Murray, 97
Fox, Dixon Ryan, 94
Freeman, Joseph, 4 n.

Gallatin, Albert, 37
Garland, Hamlin, 143, 144
Garrison, William Lloyd, 91, 142
Gates, Frederick T., 67
Gentry, the, 83–119 *passim*; as a class, 83–88, 95–96, 100, 107, 119; and cultural ideals, 87, 100; distinguished from social-economic elite, 83, 88–95, 100, 102, 106; eighteenth-century, 93–94, 96, 99, 100, 102, 112; family heritage, 96, 113; family life of, 110–14; and "natural gentlemen," 103–5, 117; overlap with social-economic elite, 96–97; regional cultural heritage of, 106–9, 112, 113, 119
Gibbon, Edward, 130
Gibbs, Josiah Willard, 41, 44, 48–50, 64, 69, 79, 131; biographies of, by Rukeyser and Wheeler, 49–50

Gilman, Daniel Coit, 46, 64, 65, 66, 80
Grant, Robert, 98
Grant, Ulysses S., 37
Gray, Asa, 59, 62
Gray, Francis Calley, 67

Hall, G. Stanley, 66, 78
Halleck, Fitz-Greene, 90
Hamilton, Alexander, 153
Harper, William Rainey, 65
Harper's Magazine, 91
Harris, Frank, 98
Hart, Albert Bushnell, 136, 152
Harvard University, 44, 51, 56, 79, 132
Hawthorne, Nathaniel, 8, 15, 144
Hay, John, 38, 41
Hegel, Georg Wilhelm Friedrich, 126
Hicks, Granville, 4 n.
Hicks, John D., 145
History: Charles Francis Adams on, 129; Henry Adams on, 130–31; Charles M. Andrews on, 129; George Bancroft on, 125; Geoffrey Barraclough on, 153–54; common factors with literature, 154–59; as different from literature, 145–52; Emerson on, 125; Kennan on, 138, 157–58; limitations on, 156–59; as literary art, vii, 139–40; Macaulay on, 124; Allan Nevins on, 137–38; and problems of dealing with recent past, ix, 3, 7–27; problems of nineteenth-century American cultural history, 33 ff.; problems in research in history of American science, 60–62; Otto Ranke on, 127, 135; relationships of, with literature, 123–26, 138–44; "scientific" versus "literary," 126–38; Theodore Roosevelt on, 132, 134–35
"History" (Emerson), 125
"History as a Literary Art" (Morison), 139–40
"History as Literature" (Roosevelt), 134–35
History of the United States During the Administrations of Jefferson and Madison (Adams), 131
Hoar, E. R., 45
Hoar, George Frisbie, 107–8
Holmes, Rev. Abiel, 96
Holmes, Oliver Wendell, 58, 59, 62, 96–97, 98
Holst, Hermann von, 136
Home Journal (N.Y.), 92
Howe, Julia Ward, 91, 99
Howe, Samuel Gridley, 91
Howells, William Dean, 78, 98, 115–18, 141
Huck Finn, 143
Hume, David, 54
Huxley, Aldous, 7

"Imagination in History" (Hart), 136
Intruder in the Dust (Faulkner), 147–48
Irving, Washington, 90

Jackson, Andrew, 104–5
James, Henry (1811–1882), 39–77
James, Henry (1843–1916), 8, 12, 39–40, 42, 49, 77, 78, 80, 143, 152
James, William, 80
Jefferson, Thomas, 84–85, 150

John Brown's Body (Benét), 152
Johnson, Robert Underwood, 110
Jordan, David Starr, 66
Josephson, Matthew, 4 n., 43, 53

Kazin, Alfred, 4 n.
Kennan, George, 138, 157–58, 159
King, Clarence, 38, 40–41, 80

Langley, Samuel Pierpont, 79
Larcom, Lucy, 108–9
Laus Deo! (Whittier), 142
Lawrence, Abbott, 65
Lazzaroni, 44–45, 48, 63, 72, 73;
    see also "Order of Scientific
    Lazzaroni"
Leatherstocking, 104, 117
*Letter to American Teachers of
    History* (Adams), 135–36
Lewis, Sinclair, 141
Life of Reason (Santayana), 75–
    76
Lincoln, Abraham, 141
Literature: as contrasted with
    history, vii, ix, x; leftism in,
    3–4, 6, 11–14, 21–24; use of,
    by historians, viii, ix, x, xi;
    value of, to historian, 141–45;
    see also History
Lodge, Henry Cabot, 38–39, 41,
    50
Long, Huey, 151
Longfellow, Henry Wadsworth,
    58, 87, 90, 144
Lowell, James Russell, 51, 55,
    56, 58, 75, 98
Lowell, John Amory, 65, 67
Lowell, Robert, 149, 152

McCarthyism, 6, 11
Macaulay, Thomas Babington,
    124–25

MacDonald, Dwight, 4 n.
Martineau, Harriet, 83, 89
Matthews, Brander, 132–33
Meinecke, Friedrich, 24
Melville, Herman, 8, 90, 144, 152
Moby-Dick (Melville), 53, 152
Mommsen, Theodore, 138
Morison, Samuel Eliot, 139–40
Motley, John Lothrop, 127, 132
Mumford, Lewis, 20–21

National Academy of Sciences,
    45, 72
Nevins, Allan, 137–38
New Haven, Conn., 45, 48, 79
New York, N.Y., 73, 90, 92, 98,
    99, 102, 141
New York (State), 102, 109, 112
New York Times, 18
Newcomb, Simon, 79
Newport, R.I., 39, 47, 73
Norris, Frank, 143
North American Review, 101
Norton, Charles Eliot, 39, 66
Notes of a Son and Brother
    (James), 39
Notions of the Americans
    (Cooper), 85

O'Connor, Flannery, 141
Octopus, The (Norris), 143
O'Hara, John, 141
"Order of Scientific Lazzaroni,"
    44–45; see also Lazzaroni
O'Reilly, John Boyle, 98

Palfrey, John Gorham, 86
Papyrus Club (Boston), 98
Parker, Theodore, 91
Parkman, Francis, 127, 128, 130,
    133

Parrington, Vernon Louis, 43, 53
Past Recaptured, The (Proust), 147
Patten, Simon, 78
Peirce, Charles Sanders, 44–48
Philadelphia (Penna.), 45, 73, 99
Phillips, Ulrich B., 143
Pierce, Banjamin, 44, 45, 46, 47, 67, 72
Pit, The (Norris), 143
Plessy v. *Ferguson*, 143
Poe, Edgar Allan, 90, 99
Powell, John Wesley, 41, 66, 67, 69, 79
Pragmatism, 44
Prescott, William Hickling, 127, 132
Proust, Marcel, 146–47
"Psalm of Life" (Longfellow), 144
Pudd'nhead Wilson (Twain), 143
Putnam, F. W., 66, 79

Quentin Durward (Scott), 127
Quincy, Josiah, 104–5

Ranke, Leopold von, 126, 127, 130, 135
Red Badge of Courage, The (Crane), 144
Redskins, The (Cooper), 103
Remsen, Ira, 79
Reichmann, Eva, 27
Roberts, Kenneth, 152
Rockefeller, John D., 66, 67
Rogers, William Barton, 59
Roosevelt, Theodore, 69; as historian, 130, 132–34, 135
Ross, E. A., 78
Royce, Josiah, 34, 77, 78, 79
Rukeyser, Muriel, 49–50

Salvimini, Gaetano, 156
Samuels, Ernest, 36
Santayana, George, 35, 44, 55, 64, 75–77, 79, 80
Saturday Club (Boston), 45, 58, 66, 73
Sartre, Jean Paul, 146
Schlesinger, Arthur M., 145
Sense of the Past (James), 8
Scott, Sir Walter, 86, 110, 124–25, 127, 130
Sears, Mrs. J. Montgomery, 98
"Self-Reliance" (Emerson), 143
Shakespeare, William, 108, 156
Sheffield Scientific School, 79
Sidgwick, Henry, 34
Sidney, Sir Philip, 86
Simpson, "Sockless" Jerry, 144
Sloane, William, 137
Smithsonian Institution, 45
Social Science Research Council, 123
"Song of Myself" (Whitman), 8
Sparks, Jared, 86
Stanford, Leland, 66, 67
Stimson, Frederick J., 97–98
Stowe, Harriet Beecher, 90, 114, 141
Sumner, Charles, 45, 72–73

Thoreau, Henry David, 47, 145
Ticknor, George, 68
Towle, George Makepeace, 98
Transcendentalism, 44
Tudor, William, 101
Turner, Frederick Jackson, 78
Twain, Mark, 53, 77, 79, 118, 143, 146
Two Years Before the Mast (Dana), 152

INDEX

Uncle Tom's Cabin (Stowe), 141
"Under the Lion's Paw" (Garland), 143–44
United States Coast Survey, 45, 46, 47

Veblen, Thorstein, 47, 66, 71, 78
Virginia, 112

War of 1812, 94
Ward, John William, 145
Ward, Lester Frank, 78
Warner, W. Lloyd, 112
Warren, Robert Penn, 150–51
Washington, D.C., 36, 40–41, 44, 45, 73, 79
Watts, Isaac, 108
Wendell, Barrett, 104, 119
Wendell, Oliver, 96

Wharton, Edith, 90–91, 92, 99, 141
Whipple, Edwin P., 68
White, Andrew Dixon, 46, 65, 66
Whitman, Walt, 8, 12, 141, 146
Whittier, John Greenleaf, 141–42
Williams, Robin, 114
Willis, Nathaniel Parker, 92–93, 98
Wilson, Edmund, 4 n.
Wilson, Henry, 45
Wilson, Woodrow, 33, 78
Winning of the West (Roosevelt), 132–34
Wordsworth, William, 109
Wright, Chauncey, 78

Xenophon, 140

Yeoman class, 104